Series / Number 07-004

TESTS OF SIGNIFICANCE

RAMON E. HENKEL
University of Maryland

SAGE PUBLICATIONS
The International Professional Publishers
Newbury Park   London   New Delhi

For information address:

SAGE Publications, Inc.
2455 Teller Road
Newbury Park, California 91320
E-mail: order@sagepub.com

SAGE Publications Ltd.
6 Bonhill Street
London EC2A 4PU
United Kingdom

SAGE Publications India Pvt. Ltd.
M-32 Market
Greater Kailash I
New Delhi 110 048 India

Printed in the United States of America

International Standard Book Number 0-8039-0652-8

Library of Congress Catalog Card No. L.C. 76-25673

00   01   26   25   24   23

When citing a university paper, please use the proper form. Remember to cite the Sage University Paper series title and include the paper number. One of the following formats can be adapted (depending on the style manual used):

(1) HENKEL, RAMON E. (1976) Tests of Significance. Sage University Paper Series on Quantitative Applications in the Social Sciences, 07-004. Newbury Park, CA: Sage.

OR

(2) Henkel, R. E. (1976). *Tests of significance* (Sage University Paper Series on Quantitative Applications in the Social Sciences, series no. 07-04). Newbury Park, CA: Sage.

CONTENTS

107060

RAMON E. HENKEL, associate professor of sociology at the University of Maryland, received his doctorate degree from the University of Wisconsin. Associate editor of the Pacific Sociological Review, Dr. Henkel is also co-editor of The Significance Test Controversy (1970).

Editor's Introduction

TESTS OF SIGNIFICANCE—one of the most fundamental and elementary forms of statistical analysis—is also one of the oldest. In 1734, the father and son Swiss mathematicians, Daniel and John Bernoulli, considered the mystery that the orbital planes of the planets are unaccountably close together. Is this closeness greater than would be expected if the orbits were *randomly* determined? The Bernoullis first worked out what is meant by randomness and then computed the *probability* that the orbital planes would be as close as indeed they had been observed (a TEST OF SIGNIFICANCE). Since the resulting probability was very small, they deduced that a physical cause was responsible.

Since the days of the Bernoullis, TESTS OF SIGNIFICANCE have become viable ways to use statistics to examine an hypothesis in light of observations. Starting with observations (the closeness of planets, the television habits of children, the voting patterns of farmers), an hypothesis is constructed about the chance mechanism generating the observations. A test statistic is formed from the observations, leading to verification or rejection of the hypothesis.

In this paper, Ramon E. Henkel discusses the basic elements of probability theory as applied to TESTS OF SIGNIFICANCE, including simple examples based on the roll of a pair of dice to demonstrate general application of this technique to any area subject to statistical analysis. He compares alternative tests on the basis of their special purposes and demonstrates how the same data might lead to varying results by using different tests. As he indicates, TESTS OF SIGNIFICANCE do not allow statements about the *strength* of associations, but only about probable relationships. For this reason, the value of TESTS OF SIGNIFICANCE has become the subject of controversy. Dr. Henkel explores these issues, presenting both sides of the debate on the utility and appropriateness of significance testing.

Among those social scientists who accept the validity of TESTS OF SIGNIFICANCE, the tests are used for a broad variety of purposes:

- A political scientist might pose the question of whether Democratic party identifiers vote more or less frequently than Republican party identifiers, or how they compare with the total set of voters. Or he could inquire as to whether there is a relationship greater than mere chance between a citizen's national origins and his political views.

● An economist or an administrator would find frequent uses for significance tests. Dr. Henkel explains their import to decision theorists. Quality control questions are often resolved by this logic: for example, a company has manufacturing procedures that result in one faulty product or less per thousand products made, yet in a sample of a thousand items, five are found unacceptable. This may result from a faulty or atypical sample—or it may indicate the *possibility* that the production process is askew.

● A psychologist or an educator might examine a group of college students and a group of midshipmen who have taken a proficiency test and determine the possibility that the two groups are more similar than random chance would allow; the similarities between the two groups might suggest that they are theoretically parts of the same population.

● A sociologist might focus on the extent of religious involvement and juvenile delinquency rates, two of the illustrations included in this paper.

But perhaps the most important application of TESTS OF SIGNIFICANCE is simply that it is a fundamental tool for reading more advanced material. It is important to understand the logic behind significance testing before reading some of the other papers in this series, particularly those on *Analysis of Variance** and *Analysis of Covariance,*** as well as the two papers on regression analysis*** which assume a knowledge of TESTS OF SIGNIFICANCE and discuss it in more sophisticated detail.

—E. M. Uslaner, Series Editor

*Gudmund R. Iversen and Helmut Norpoth (1976) *Analysis of Variance.* Sage University Papers in Quantitative Applications in the Social Sciences, series no. 07-001. Beverly Hills and London: Sage Publications.

**A. R. Wildt and O. T. Ohtola (forthcoming) *Analysis of Covariance.* Sage University Papers in Quantitative Applications in the Social Sciences. Beverly Hills and London: Sage Publications.

***Eric Uslaner (forthcoming) *Regression Analysis: Simultaneous Equation Estimation* and Charles Ostrom (forthcoming) *Regression Analysis: Time Series Analysis,* both in the Sage University Papers in Quantitative Applications in the Social Sciences. Beverly Hills and London: Sage Publications.

TESTS OF SIGNIFICANCE

RAMON E. HENKEL
University of Maryland

1. OVERVIEW

Tests of significance are widely used in social science research. Yet there is considerable difference of opinion on their value in achieving the goals of science. In the author's opinion, the tests are of little or no value in basic social science research, where basic research is identified as that which is directed toward the development and validation of theory. On the other hand, tests of significance seem to be of value in research which is directed toward the solution of immediate practical problems where a decision must be made, and resources allocated on the basis of the decision. However, it is also the author's opinion that one is in a position to make a rational decision about the utility of tests of significance in basic research *only* when one understands them thoroughly. It is the objective of this paper to provide the information needed to understand the conceptual and logical basis for tests of significance, and thus provide the basis for the reader's personal decision as to the utility of significance tests in his or her research.

Understanding tests of significance involves at least the following: acquiring the technical information, skills, and extensive technical vocabulary needed for a mastery of the calculational aspects of the tests; acquiring an understanding of the questions for which tests of significance provide partial answers; and acquiring a sense of the nature of the information bearing on these questions which the tests provide. As prerequisites to obtaining this knowledge and these skills, one needs a minimal level of arithmetic and algebraic skills, an elementary knowledge of descriptive techniques—measures of central tendency, variability, and relation—some knowledge of probability theory, some knowledge of sampling procedures, and some knowledge of logic and philosophy of science—the latter particularly in conjunction with the logic and interpretation of tests of significance.

It is assumed that the readers of this paper will have the basic tool skills of arithmetic and algebra. Since the length of the paper precludes a presentation of descriptive statistics, it is also assumed that the reader has an elementary knowledge of descriptive statistics—at least the ability to calculate means, sums of squares, correlation and regression coefficients, and some elementary nonparametric measures of strength of relationship. Elements of probability theory, sampling, and philosophy of science will be presented at appropriate points in the paper.

2. STATISTICS

Before considering tests of significance in detail, it is useful to take a broader look at statistics to see where significance testing fits into the array of statistical techniques.

Statistical techniques are usually characterized as being either descriptive or inferential. Descriptive techniques present information contained in a set of data in some summary form—tables, graphs, summary numbers such as means, variances, measures of relationship, factors and factor loadings, discriminant functions, and the like. Inferential techniques are used to evaluate or characterize the manner in which chance factors in the selection of a subset of data (sample) affect descriptions of, or conclusions about, the larger set of data (population) from which we selected the subset. Statistical inference involves procedures which either allow us to characterize a population on the basis of a sample, and state how good this characterization is, or decide how well a sample fits our preconceptions of the population from which we drew the sample.

Inferential techniques are characterized as either estimation or hypothesis testing procedures, with estimation procedures resulting in either point or interval estimates. Estimates are usually employed when we are ignorant of characteristics of the data and are descriptive statistics in the sense that they describe the sample. They are inferential in the sense that not only are they considered descriptive of the cases examined, but also of the unexamined cases in the population from which they were drawn. Point estimates are single values such as means, variances, measures of relationship, and the like. Interval estimates are ranges of values, usually centered on a point estimate, that indicate, in a sense, bounds within which we expect the true value for the whole population to lie.

Hypothesis testing (significance testing), on the other hand, is employed to test some assumption (hypothesis) we have about the population against a sample from the population. In a sense to be explored in detail later, the result of a significance test is a probability which we attach to a descriptive statistic calculated from a sample. This probability reflects how likely it is that the statistic could have come from a sample drawn from the population specified in the hypothesis.

Common Sense Perspective on Statistics

Statistics is based on common sense. If the complexity of some of the formulas and procedures is stripped away, and the technical vocabulary is replaced by more commonly used expressions, statistics is a very common sense approach to obtaining information through the manipulation of numbers.

From a common sense perspective, testing a particular belief or assumption (which we can call a hypothesis) follows a pattern. We assume something (the hypothesis) to be true, and we test this hypothesis by comparing observations (data) on the real world with what our hypothesis would lead us to expect. If what we find in the real world corresponds closely enough with what our hypothesis led us to expect, we continue to believe our hypothesis. If, on the other hand, what we observe does not correspond closely enough to what we expect, we suspect our hypothesis of being false, and may reject it, or reformulate it.

For example, suppose we believe that a particular coin we have is "fair," that is, if flipped it should land heads half of the time and tails the other half. Following our common sense inclinations, we decide to test the hypothesis of fairness by flipping the coin several times. Keeping track of the results we find that in 20 flips of the coin it turned heads 14 times. What do we decide? Without some specific criteria of what constitutes a close enough fit between what we expect on the basis of our hypothesis— in this case, 10 heads— and what we observe, it is not clear what we would decide about the fairness of the coin. Some of us may decide that the coin is fair, and that 14 heads—four more than expected—just represents what can happen in the short run when flipping a fair coin. Others of us may decide that the coin is not fair, and that it is more reasonable to believe that the probability of getting a head in a single flip is not .5, but rather something like .6 or .7. Without more specific criteria of closeness, or without more information, it is likely that the experiment would be viewed as inconclusive by many others.

In situations similar to the coin flipping experiment, we will come to some conclusion based on a subjective evaluation of whether or not our results were close to what we expected—including the possibility that we may want to suspend judgment until we get more information. Unfortunately, what we may take as "close" in such situations is quite variable. Our own subjective evaluation may change from day to day, and our subjective evaluation is likely to be different from that of others who may evaluate the same information.

Formal Criteria

Significance testing is assumed to offer an advantage over subjective evaluations of closeness in contexts such as that illustrated above *where there are no specific criteria* for what constitutes enough agreement (between our expectations and our observations) to allow us to continue to believe our hypothesis, or constitutes great enough divergence to lead us to suspect that our hypothesis is false. In a general sense, tests of significance, as one approach to assessing our beliefs or assumptions about reality, differ from the common sense approach only in the degree to which the criterion for closeness of, or correspondence between, observed and expected results are formalized, that is, specific and standardized across tests. Significance testing allows us to evaluate differences between what we expect on the basis of our hypothesis, and what we observe, but only in terms of one criterion, the probability that these differences could have occurred by "chance."

The source of differences which significance testing allows us to evaluate are called *chance factors,* or *random factors,* and *from the statistician's point of view, the only sources of chance factors which will be considered are those associated with the manner in which the observations used to test hypotheses are selected.* Though we will not define chance, or random, factors there are certain characteristics we associate with them—the specific factors affecting a particular outcome are *unknown, numerous, independent,* and generally *lead to equally likely outcomes* for the phenomena affected. What we mean by chance factors and the effect of chance factors is illustrated in a fairly simple fashion by a number of gambling devices and games. For example, the roll of a pair of dice illustrates the notion of random factors. Many factors associated with the roll of a pair of dice affect the result—how hard they are rolled, the initial position of the dice, how they hit the surface on which they are rolled, and so on—though we do not know which, or how many of these factors affect a particular roll. Yet, as a result of these factors we assign an equal probability to each of the six faces of a die.

Though it may seem paradoxical, by assuming that chance factors affect phenomena, and by making certain assumptions about the manner in which chance factors affect phenomena (essentially that they are independent, and produce equally likely outcomes), we can derive the distribution of outcomes of particular phenomena. In other words, we can determine the relative frequency with which each possible result, or outcome, will occur. In the case of two dice, there are 36 possible outcomes for a roll (each face on one die may be paired with any one of the six faces on the other die) though there are only 11 possible sums for the spots on the faces. By assuming that only chance factors can affect the outcome of a roll of a pair of dice, and applying the rules for probability calculations, we can determine the relative frequency with which each of the possible 11 totals will occur in a very long series of rolls of the dice. Thus, assuming that only chance factors affect the outcome of a roll allows us to deduce a long run regularity of the phenomena, though this information is of no use in predicting what will happen on any one particular roll of the dice.

In tests of significance we assume our hypothesis to be true. On the basis of this hypothesis and the further assumption that the only factors which would produce observations different from what was hypothesized are chance factors, we derive a distribution of possible outcomes (analogous to the 11 possible totals of the two faces on the dice) which gives us the relative frequency with which those outcomes would occur. Given the hypothesis, the assumption that only chance factors are affecting what we observe, and the distribution of outcomes based on the assumption of the workings of chance factors, we can determine how likely it is—the probability—that any particular observation would occur. It is *only* in this sense that significance testing allows us to evaluate differences between what we expected and what we observed. In other words, it is only in terms of a probability that we assess differences between observations and expectations. Our procedures in significance testing will allow us only to evaluate the likelihood (or probability) of our results (observations) under the *combined assumptions of the truth of our hypothesis and the effects of chance factors.* If the differences between what we expected on the basis of our hypothesis and what we observed could be attributed to chance factors, we would continue to believe our hypothesis. If the difference is too great to be attributed to chance factors, our conclusion would be to doubt the truth of the hypothesis.

Although significance testing provides criteria for determining when expectations and observations are in agreement or disagreement by considering the effect of chance factors in a rigorous fashion, it does not completely eliminate the subjective aspects of making this assessment. Subjective judgments are still a part of the process, since the choice of the probability which will lead to a decision that the hypothesis is false is an arbitrary, subjective choice. Thus tests of significance introduce a certain amount of rigor, and eliminate a certain amount of subjectivity, but do not remove all subjectivity from the process.

3. CONCEPTUAL FRAMEWORK

For a rigorous discussion of tests of significance, it is necessary to develop an elementary knowledge of probability and a technical vocabulary. The introduction of this material, particularly the necessary terminology, will involve a rather extended portion of this paper.

Populations, Parameters, Samples, and Statistics

Statistical inference deals with populations and samples from populations. A *population* is any well defined collection or set of values, such as the values on some variable of interest. This sense of the term "population" differs from the sense in which most social scientists use the term, as social scientists tend to view collections of people, laboratory animals, and the like as populations. Thus the social scientist's population, typically, gives rise to many populations in the statistician's sense, since the social scientist thinks in terms of measures on a series of variables (populations) for each case in his population of people, laboratory animals, and the like. This different sense of "population" is potentially a source of some problems in applying and interpreting tests of significance (Gold, 1969). A *sample* is any subset of values from a population.

Statistical inference is a process by which we make inferences (generalizations) about population parameters on the basis of sample statistics. A *parameter* is a value characterizing a population. Examples of parameters are the mean of the population, the variance of the population, the correlation between two variables, and the like. A *sample statistic*, or *statistic*, is a value for an equivalent characteristic of a sample, and such sample statistics are usually considered estimates of the population characteristics.

Probability

Since tests of significance, like all statistical inference, are based in probability theory, we need to indicate what we mean by "probability."

Though there are other interpretations of the term the sense in which probability is used in this paper is the relative frequency sense.[1] What this means is that if we take some particular event, say the flip of a coin, the probability of a particular outcome, say heads, is the number of times that particular outcome occurs divided by the number of flips. If we designate a particular outcome as a success (s), and all others as failures (f), where s + f is the total number of trials (flips), we would symbolize the probability of success as

$$P(s) = s/(s + f).$$

Similarly, we would symbolize the probability of a failure as

$$P(f) = f/(s + f).$$

It follows from these that the probability of either a success or a failure is

$$P(s) + P(f) = s/(s + f) + f/(s + f) = (s + f)/(s + f) = 1.$$

It also follows from these ideas that probabilities can never be negative, and that probabilities must be in the range of zero to one ($0 \leqslant P(s) \leqslant 1$). If the probability of a particular outcome is established on the basis of observation it is called an *empirical probability*. If the probability of a particular outcome is established on the basis of assumptions (such as the assumption of equally likely outcomes) and rules for combining probabilities, it is called a *theoretical* or *mathematical probability*. However, in either case, the probability is viewed as a relative frequency, and refers to what would occur in the long run. (Empirical probabilities calculated on the basis of a few trials are generally considered tentative and subject to revision in the light of additional trials.) As examples we would consider that the probability of a male birth is about .51 as a statement of an empirical probability, since the basis for the probability calculation is the observed proportion of births which are male. We would consider the statement that the probability of a seven in a single roll of two fair dice is .167 as a statement of a theoretical or mathematical probability, as the probability is obtained on the basis of the fact that six of the 36 possible, equally likely outcomes of the roll of two fair dice given seven as a total (6/36 = .167). Though it is repetitious, it is important to remember that as used here, probabilities refer to relative frequencies over the long run since it is in this sense of probability that we will interpret the results of tests of significance.[2]

One of the more important concepts from probability theory relevant to tests of significance is the notion of a random variable. As used here, a *random variable* is a variable for which we know the probability density function or probability distribution, and whose observed values are the outcome of the action of chance factors.[3] In other words a random variable has the characteristics that though we cannot predict the next value of the variable to be observed, we know the relative frequency with which each possible value will occur in the long run. Also, the term "variable" in this context refers, typically, to some statistic (such as a sum, a mean, a correlation, a standard score, or the like) rather than to some substantive variable (such as status, political party preference, race, or the like). A simple example of a random variable is the set of outcomes of the rolls of a pair of dice. The values of the random variable are the sums obtained by adding the values on the faces of the two dice. Though we cannot predict the sum which will occur on any particular roll of the dice, by assuming each face of a die has an equal probability of turning up and by using the rules for combining probabilities (see below), we can calculate the relative frequency for the various sums which can occur in the rolls of a pair of dice.

The relative frequency distribution for the outcomes of the rolls of the dice illustrate another important concept, the notion of a *probability distribution*. The important characteristics of a probability distribution are:

(1) It represents all the theoretically possible values of the random variable.

(2) It indicates the probability of each of the theoretically possible values occurring on any trial.

(3) The sum of the probabilities in the distribution is 1. (Another way of expressing the same information is in terms of area; the area under the graph of the probability distribution is one unit.)

Table 1 is the probability distribution for the outcomes of rolls of a pair of dice. The theoretically possible values are the sums (scores) 2 through 12, the probability for each of the sums is given, and the probabilities sum to 1. Figure 1 is the graph of this probability distribution. The area in each column of the histogram represents the probability of getting the indicated sum, or outcome. Thus various probabilities can be found either by adding the correct probabilities from Table 1, or by combining the correct areas from Figure 1 since these are equivalent procedures. For example, the probability of getting one of several specified

TABLE 1
Probability Distribution for the Outcomes of a Single Roll
of a Pair of Dice

Score	probability (p)		
2	1/36	=	.02778
3	2/36	=	.05556
4	3/36	=	.08333
5	4/36	=	.11111
6	5/36	=	.13889
7	6/36	=	.16667
8	5/36	=	.13889
9	4/36	=	.11111
10	3/36	=	.08333
11	2/36	=	.05556
12	1/36	=	.02778
	36/36	=	1.00000

outcomes, say either 10, 11, or 12, is obtained by adding the areas in these three columns (.083 + .056 + .028 = .167). Since the total area under the graph is 36/36ths or 1, the probability of getting either 10, 11, or 12 can be obtained another way. The areas for the outcomes 0, 1, 2, . . . , 9 can be added, and this total subtracted from 1, that is,

$$1 - (.028 + .056 + \ldots + .011) = .167.$$

The concept of an expected value plays an important part in probability theory and statistics. An *expected value*, symbolized as E(X)—where X is a random variable—is simply the mean of the random variable, and for discrete probability distributions, can be found from the formula

$$E(X) = \Sigma p_i X_i$$

where p_i is the probability of getting the value X_i. Thus the expected value for the probability distribution in Table 1 is seven. In other words, in a long series of rolls of a pair of dice, we would expect an average score of 7. Earlier it was stated that assuming that only chance factors affected outcomes for some phenomenon allowed us to derived the relative frequency, or probability, distribution for those outcomes, and that tests of signifi-

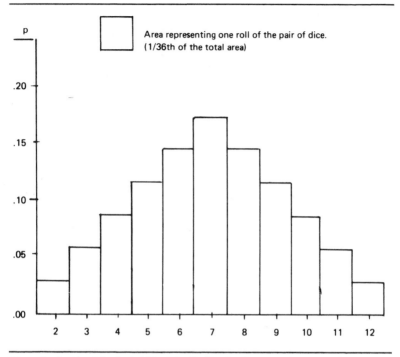

Figure 1: Graph of the Probability Distribution for Scores on One Roll of a Pair of Dice

cance would allow us to determine whether the difference between what we observed and what we expected could be explained by "chance." As will be seen later, "what we expected" will usually be the expected value of the probability distribution of the outcomes for the phenomenon. In other words, what we expect is what would happen on the average.

Since the interpretation of probability underlying most statistical usage is the relative frequency interpretation, an important concept is the notion of a sample space (sometimes called a sample description space, or possibility set). A *sample space* is simply the complete listing of all possible outcomes of some phenomenon. Its relevance to the frequency interpretation of probability is that the probability of any particular outcome is obtained by counting. The number of outcomes representing a success, as well as the total number of outcomes, can be obtained by counting, and the probability of a success can then be obtained by taking the ratio of the number of successes to the total number of outcomes.

For example, suppose a fair coin—one for which the probability of either a head (H) or a tail (T) is .5—is tossed three times. The sample space for the outcomes is

HHH	TTT
HHT	TTH
HTH	THT
HTT	THH

From this list we can obtain probabilities for various outcomes. For example, the probability of obtaining three heads in three tosses is 1/8, since there are eight possible outcomes, and only one of these is the required three successive heads. Similarly, the possibility of getting two heads in three tosses is 3/8, since three of the outcomes contain two heads.

The notion of a sample space is also useful in developing the concept of conditional probability, which in turn is useful in developing the much used concept of independence. A *conditional probability* is one in which additional information is employed to revise the "unconditional" probability. For any two outcomes A and B, the conditional probability of B, given that A has occurred—symbolized $P(B|A)$, where the vertical bar means "on the condition that"—is calculated as a relative frequency, but the sample space is now reduced to those cases involving the occurrence of A.

For example, the (conditional) probability of getting two heads in three tosses given that the result on the first toss is a head is found by considering the subset of the sample space in which a head appeared on the first toss (the first column of the sample space listing above). There are four such outcomes, and two of these contain two heads. Thus P(two heads in three tosses|head on first toss) = .5. Similarly, P(two heads in three tosses|tail on first toss) = .25. These two cases illustrate the fact that conditional probabilities can be larger and smaller than the unconditional probability (which was 3/8ths).

Given the notion of conditional probability, we can indicate what we mean when we say that two outcomes A and B are independent. A and B are independent when

$$P(B|A) = P(B)$$
$$P(A|B) = P(A)$$

In other words, two outcomes are *independent* if the fact that one of them has occurred has no effect on the probability that the second will occur.

For example, we would conclude that the tosses of a coin are independent if the probability of both heads and tails remained constant (.5) irrespective of what turned up on the preceding toss. An examination of the sample space indicates that this, theoretically, is the case, as half of the time a head is followed by a tail, the other half of the time a head is followed by a head, and the same pattern holds for tails.

Though all probability calculations can theoretically be reduced to counts based on sample spaces, in most nontrivial probability calculations it becomes too cumbersome to actually obtain the entire sample space. Thus a considerable portion of probability theory is concerned with procedures for obtaining information on relevant portions of the sample space—for example, the number of successful outcomes and the total number of outcomes—while another portion is concerned with the direct calculation of probabilities of particular outcomes by application of rules for combining probabilities.

Though we will not present any of the procedures for obtaining information on a sample space, we will present two of the most commonly used rules for combining probabilities, and show how they can be used to obtain a probability distribution (the probability distribution for the rolls of a pair of dice) without, in a sense, obtaining the sample space of the outcomes.

The two rules are usually called the addition rule and the multiplication rule. The *addition rule* states that the probability of either of two *mutually exclusive* outcomes occurring is the sum of their separate probabilities. Thus for two outcomes A and B,

$$P(A \text{ or } B) = P(A) + P(B).$$

The *multiplication rules* states that the probability of two *independent* outcomes occurring simultaneously is the product of their separate probabilities. Thus for two outcomes A and B,

$$P(A \text{ and } B) = P(A)P(B).$$

As an illustration of these rules, we can find the probability of a particular score, say 8, on a single roll of a pair of dice. To find the probability of a particular configuration on the dice which gives this score, say a 3 on the first and a 5 on the second, we use the multiplication rule. Assuming that the results on one of the dice is independent of the results on the other and that the faces are equiprobable, we get the required probability from the following calculation:

$$P(3 \text{ and } 5) = P(3)P(5) = (1/6)(1/6) = 1/36.$$

However, a score of 8 can be obtained in a number of different ways—five to be exact—so to get the probability for a score of 8 we need to use the addition rule. Each of the five configurations of the dice giving 8, $(3+5, 5+3, 2+6, 6+2, 4+4)$, are mutually exclusive—only one of the five can occur in a single roll—thus the required probability is the sum of the separate probabilities:

$$P(\text{score of } 8) = P(2 \text{ and } 6) + P(6 \text{ and } 2) + P(3 \text{ and } 5) + \ldots$$
$$+ P(4 \text{ and } 4) = (1/36) + (1/36) + \ldots + (1/36) = 5/36.$$

Applying these two rules successively to the scores 2 through 12 results in the probability distribution given in Table 1.

Though it would be foolish to expect this brief introduction to probability theory to provide a basis for even most simple probability calculations, the ideas presented provide some background for understanding the conceptual framework of significance testing.

Sampling Distributions

One of the most basic concepts in statistical inference is the notion of a sampling distribution. It brings together the notions of random variable and probability distribution. A *sampling distribution* is a theoretical probability distribution which represents all the possible values we could obtain for a sample statistic and the relative frequency (probability) with which these values would occur in the long run when drawing the appropriate probability samples of size N from a specified population. (We will defer until later the discussion of what constitutes a proper probability sampling procedure.) Under these assumptions (proper probability sample, specified population) various statistics calculated from the samples can be treated as random variables.[4] An important point relating to the interpretation of significance tests lies in the relation between sampling procedures, chance factors, and the ability to treat sample statistics as random variables. That point is that the source of the chance factors which allow us to treat sample statistics as random variables lies in the sampling process—*nowhere else*. It is the manner in which the chance factors operate in the sampling process that introduces the long run regularity in the sample statistics that result in our being able to derive the sampling distribution of the statistic.

An important characteristic of the sampling distribution of a statistic is that it is a probability distribution, based on assumptions about the population. (In other words, the sampling distribution is dependent on the population—the population has a deterministic effect on the long run of samples drawn from it on a random basis.) In addition, the sampling distribution represents all the possible values of the statistic which can occur on the basis of what is (assumed) true of the population, and the sampling distribution gives the relative frequency (probability) with which the various values of the statistic will occur in the long run.

Although sampling distributions are obtained through mathematical derivations based on assumptions about the manner in which chance factors operate, an intuitive grasp of the information contained in a sampling distribution can be obtained by considering an empirical experiment that we could perform. To use an earlier example, we could roll a pair of fair dice a large number of times, record the outcomes of each roll (sum of spots showing on the face of the dice), and graph the result. Since there are 11 different possible values that could result, each experiment would have to include a fairly large number of rolls—say 100. Each experiment of 100 rolls would produce a graph (frequency distribution) similar to Figure 1, though each graph would be somewhat different, since the short run effects of chance factors will only approximate (more or less well) the long run effects. However, if we were to repeat the experiment rolling the dice 1,000 times, the resulting relative frequency distribution would closely approximate the proportions in Figure 1. Thus the sampling distribution represents the relative frequency with which the various possible values of the sample statistic will occur in the long run, and this can be demonstrated (but not proved) by actually performing some simple experiments such as rolling dice.

Another way to look at sampling distributions is in relation to population distributions and sample distributions. If we again use the example of rolls of a pair of dice, the *population distribution*—that is, the distribution of values from which we are sampling—is a uniform distribution of six elements which are the numerals 1 through 6. The population itself can be thought of as infinite, that is, the total number of elements is infinite, but there is an equal number of each of the six numerals. Figure 2 is a histogram of the distribution of this population.

Each roll of the dice can be thought of as a sample of two ($N=2$) from this population, and the sum of the values on the two dice as the sample statistic. Each of these samples has a distribution called, naturally, a *sample distribution* to differentiate it from the population distribution. Figures 3a through 3d are histograms for four of these samples of two cases. Since the samples are so small compared to the range of possible

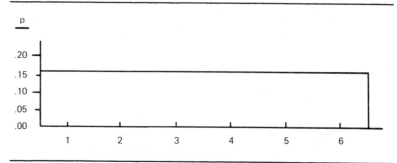

Figure 2: Graph of the Uniform Distribution for the Equiprobable Values 1 through 6

values, it is impossible for any of these sample distributions to look like the population distribution. However, even if we drew samples of 30 cases, a large proportion of such samples would be distributed in a nonuniform manner, though intuitively at least, the larger the sample, the closer the sample distribution would approximate the population distribution.

If we now turn again to Figure 1, it is clear that the graph of the sample statistic, and therefore the distribution of the sample statistic, is different from both the population and sample distributions, yet the form of presentation is identical in all three cases. The horizontal axis (abscissa) represents all the possible values which the statistic can take, and the vertical axis (ordinate) is a function of the frequency for each value. Again, the sampling distribution presents the theoretical probability distribution of some random variable (sample statistic) calculated from a sample of a given number (N) of cases. The resulting sampling distribution may be discrete, as in Figure 1, or it may be continuous. Even if the sampling distribution is discrete, for reasons of economy of time and effort in calculations, we may in many instances *approximate* it with an easier to calculate continuous distribution.

If we had calculated some other statistic, say the variance, from our samples rather than the sum of the values, the sampling distribution of this statistic would be different from the distribution of sums. Each different statistic calculated for samples from a population will have a sampling distribution, and this distribution, in general, will be different from the distribution of the other statistics.

To summarize, in statistical inference we are concerned with three types of distributions—population distributions, sample distributions, and sampling distributions. The distribution of the population has an effect on the distribution of samples drawn from it, and on the distribution of sample statistics, though for certain robust[5] parametric statistics and

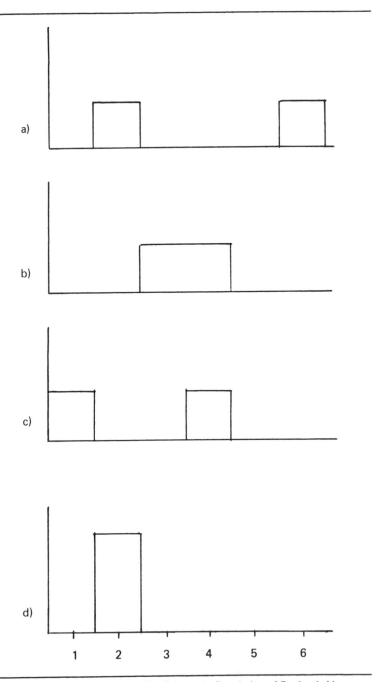

Figure 3: Graphs of Samples of 2 (N=2) from the Population of Equiprobable
Values 1 through 6

most nonparametric statistics, this effect is of little consequence. However, the sampling distribution for many techniques is based on the assumption that the population is distributed in a specific fashion, so unless it is known that the technique is robust with regard to the assumption of population distribution, it is likely that the sampling distribution is affected, and probability calculations based on that sampling distribution will be in error. Of the three distributions, the most critical to statistical inference and consequently to tests of significance is the sampling distribution. *If it is not known, inference is impossible.*

Sampling

The manner in which we select samples from our populations is critical to significance testing, since the sampling procedure determines the manner in which chance factors affect the statistic(s) we are concerned with, and consequently affect the sampling distribution of the statistic. In order to derive the sampling distribution of a statistic, we must know the manner in which chance factors affect the choice of elements from the population, thus we must draw samples on a probability basis in such a way that we "know" how chance factors work. Sampling processes are usually grouped into two broad classes—probability sampling, and nonprobability sampling. A *probability sample* is one in which chance factors determine which elements from the population will be included in the sample, and determine this in such a way that it is theoretically possible to calculate the probability that any specific element in the population becomes an element in the sample, though for practical considerations it may be difficult to make this calculation.[6]

There are several procedures which, singly or in combination, result in probability samples.[7] However, we will, for reasons to be indicated, consider only one type of probability sampling procedure—simple random sampling—in detail.

Simple random samples result when two conditions are met in selecting elements from the population. These are that each element in the population must have an equal probability of being included in the sample, and that the choice of elements must be independent. Another way of expressing these same conditions is that a simple random sample results if all possible samples of size N have an equal probability of being drawn (are equally probable). The notion of independence (defined in the section on probability) when applied to sampling, means only that the choice of an element has no effect on the choice of any other element. To illustrate the notion of independence in the sampling process, assume we want a sample of married persons containing both men and women. If we obtain the sample by working from a list which contains only the names of married men, randomly select men from the list, and then include both the man and his wife in the sample we would *not* have obtained a simple random sample. In this case the criterion of independence would not have been met, since the women included in the sample are there if, and only if, their husbands were included. This constitutes a dependence in the sampling process. Though this fact should be easy to grasp at an intuitive level, the use of the definition of independence given earlier may make the conclusion clearer. Assuming that there are N cases (men and women) in the population, each case has a probability of $1/N$ of being included in the sample if the selections are independent. However, the probability of a woman being selected, given that her husband was not selected is 0.0, and the probability of a woman being selected given that her husband was selected, is 1.0. Neither of these conditional probabilities is equal to the unconditional probability of $1/N$. Thus the selection process illustrated is not independent. On the other hand, independence would result if a single list of married persons were used, the list was a mix of both married men and married women, and elements of the sample were chosen one at a time from the list.

The reason for focusing on the notion of simple random sampling is that this is the type of sampling procedure assumed in virtually all tests of significance. This is due, mainly, to the fact that the derivation of sampling distributions is relatively easy under the assumption of simple random sampling, but difficult (to the point of being virtually impossible) to derive for more complex types of probability sampling designs, and the types of relational statistics (statistics in which two or more variables are being compared, correlated, or in some sense being simultaneously and relatively evaluated—sometimes called *analytic statistics*) commonly used in social research. In other words, most of the tests of significance given in textbooks are based on sampling distributions whose derivation is based on the assumption that the sampling process has been a simple random sampling process. In general, when the statement is made that a technique is based on the assumption that the sample is random, or has been drawn at random, what is meant is that the sample must be drawn in accordance with the requirements of independence and equal probability—in other words, the sample must be a simple random sample.

If we wish to draw a simple random sample we need, first of all, a complete list of the elements in the population. Then we need a means of drawing the sample from the list in a way that insures independence and equal probability in the choice of the elements to be included in the sample. The requirements of independence and equal probability are usually and easily met by using tables of random numbers, or other devices which provide random numbers, which are then used to select cases from the list. Unfortunately, however, there is a very serious problem in drawing simple random samples. The problem in drawing a simple random sample is that of obtaining the list of the population. Obtaining a list of a population (say, a list of some human population of interest) which is theoretically relevant is difficult because of many factors—such as the general unavailability of a list that is complete at any one time; the fact that any list, however complete at some time, is quickly outdated by births, deaths, and geographic mobility; the fact that any existing list is usually based on a small geographic area and does not include the totality of the population of theoretical interest, and so on.

As noted earlier, there are a number of sampling procedures not discussed here that result in probability samples. A discussion of these procedures has been omitted because the use of these designs poses problems for significance testing since the sampling distributions for commonly used relational statistics are generally not known for probability sampling procedures other than simple random sampling. (For a discussion of a way to ameliorate this problem, see the section on random subsampling.)

Nonprobability samples are samples drawn in such a way that the probability of an element of the population being included in the sample cannot be calculated. Since there is no way to calculate the probability of each element in the population being included in the sample, the manner in which chance factors affect the choice of elements cannot be specified, and the derivation of the sampling distribution of various statistics becomes impossible. Thus the use of statistical inference on nonprobability samples is not legitimate if the intent is to generalize *statistically* to the population sampled.

Common sampling procedures resulting in nonprobability samples are the use of captive audiences—classes of introductory sociology or psychology students, volunteers for experiments from among prison inmates, and the like—or the selection of cases from the stream of people passing a particular street corner. A common occurrence in data gathering, nonresponse, can also result in a sample which is technically a nonprobability sample, since the effect of nonresponse is to make it impossible to determine the probability of each element in the population becoming part of the sample.

Common Theoretical Distributions

There are many sampling distributions. Some of these are unique to a single technique, and others are used in a wide range of tests of significance. The more commonly used distributions are often utilized with numerous techniques. The sampling distributions most familiar to social scientists are the normal distribution, the chi-square distribution, the F-distribution, and the Student's t, or, simply, the t-distribution. In the following sections we will discuss the general characteristics of these distributions, indicate how the appropriate test statistic is calculated, and show how the sampling distribution is used to assess the probability of a particular result. Later sections will provide examples of tests of significance involving these distributions.

The normal distribution is perhaps the most used theoretical distribution because the sampling distribution of many statistics is normal or closely approximated by the normal distribution—particularly either when the sample size is large or the number of *degrees of freedom*[8] is large. The graph of the normal distribution is the bell shaped curve depicted in Figure 4. There are certain characteristics of the normal distribution worth

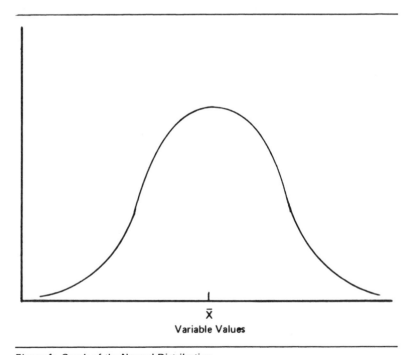

$\bar{X}$

Variable Values

Figure 4: Graph of the Normal Distribution

noting. It is completely specified by two parameters, its mean, μ, and standard deviation, σ. It is a continuous distribution. It is symmetric about its mean, and for this reason only one-half of the distribution needs to be presented—usually the upper, or positive half. The curve is asymptotic. This means that the graph extends out to infinity in both directions from the mean without the graph touching the horizontal axis. However, for all practical purposes the graph can be considered to extend only three standard deviations from the mean in each direction, as less than .0015 of the area under the curve lies beyond three standard deviations from the mean.

The *standard normal* distribution is a special case of the normal distribution. It has an area of one unit, and can therefore be used as a probability distribution. It has a mean of zero, and a standard deviation of 1. Area in the distribution is figured in terms of standard deviations and/or fractions of standard deviations from the mean. Tables for the standard normal distribution are based on standardized values, and information obtained from samples is converted (transformed) to standard form in significance tests based on the normal distribution. The required transformation is the familiar z-score transformation

$$z = [X - E(X)]/\sigma_X$$

where X is some normally distributed statistic. In other words, a z-score transformation divides the difference between a statistic and the mean (expected value) of the distribution of that statistic by the standard deviation of that statistic. The calculated z-score is the number of standard deviations the statistic is from its mean, and the table of standard normal distribution areas can be used to obtain the probability of a statistic of that value, or more extreme value, occurring as a result of sampling error assuming the hypothesis about the population is true.

The t-distribution, like the normal, is a continuous, symmetric, asymptotic distribution. However, unlike the normal distribution, it is completely specified by a single parameter, the degrees of freedom. Compared with the shape of the normal distribution, the t-distribution, for degrees of freedom less than about 120, contains more area in the tails of the distribution. For more than 120 degrees of freedom, the normal distribution approximates the t-distribution well enough that the normal distribution may be used in its place. Values of t are calculated from the following transformation

$$t = [X - E(X)]/S_X$$

where X is some t-distributed statistic, and S_x is the estimate of the standard deviation of X. Note that the t-score differs from the z-score only in that the denominator of the t-score is an estimate of the parameter while the denominator of the z-score is the parameter. Tables for the t-distribution differ from those for the normal distribution, since the t-distribution's shape changes for each degrees of freedom specified. Thus the tables for t generally give values of t such that an indicated proportion of distribution will equal or exceed the given value for each tabled degree of freedom.

The theoretical chi-square (χ^2) distribution, like the t-distribution, is specified by one parameter: the degrees of freedom. However, unlike either the normal distribution or the t-distribution, chi-square values can be only positive or zero. The chi-square distribution is continuous and skewed, though as the number of degrees of freedom becomes large, the distribution becomes more symmetric, and can be approximated by the normal distribution given appropriate formulas for the mean and standard deviation. (For *very* large degrees of freedom the mean is equal to the degrees of freedom, and the standard deviation is equal to the square root of two times the mean.)

Though formulas for calculating values of chi-square vary somewhat with application, one of the more common is

$$\chi^2 = \Sigma(O - E)^2/E$$

where O represents an observed frequency in some category of a variable and E represents an expected frequency for that category.[9] The expected value is calculated from some theoretical model appropriate to the situation, and usually in the case of bivariate distributions, the model is that the variables are independent. Specific examples of the calculation of expected values will be given later.

The theoretical F-distribution is based on the ratio of two variance estimates. The F-distribution is specified by two parameters, the two degrees of freedom—the degrees of freedom for the numerator and the degrees of freedom for the denominator of the ratio. In addition, the distribution is continuous, its values are either zero or positive, and like the chi-square distribution, it is skewed when degrees of freedom are small. The general formula for calculating an F-value is

$$F = S_1^2/S_2^2$$

where S_1^2 is one variance estimate, and S_2^2 is the second variance estimate. In order for the use of the F-distribution to be legitimate, in other words, for the resulting statistic to be random variable, the two variance estimates must be statistically independent. Statistical independence in this case means that a graph of the joint distribution of a series of such variance estimates would exhibit a random scatter of points, that is, that the variance estimates are uncorrelated.

To reiterate, as long as simple random sampling has been employed, and the populations from which the samples were drawn were normally distributed, the statistics z, t, χ^2 and F calculated for those samples are all random variables, and the theoretical sampling distributions for those *test statistics*[10] can be used to obtain the probability of a particular sample result.

Finally, it should be noted that the formulas for z, t, χ^2 and F given above *do not* define the theoretical distributions. (The formulas defining the theoretical distributions are not needed for our purposes, but the interested reader may consult a text such as Hays [1973] for details of the formulas.) What is important is that the formulas given above allow us to transform information from a sample to a form that can be used in conjunction with the theoretical sampling distributions to assess the probability of the sample result.

Using Probability Distributions

Basically, when using a probability distribution in connection with a test of significance we want

(1) to determine the probability associated with a particular value calculated from a sample;

(2) to determine—given a particular probability—the sample value associated with that probability; or

(3) to determine whether a particular sample value is more or less probable than some set probability (significance level).

These are not mutually exclusive determinations, as (1) and (2) are just the reverse of each other, and (3) involves having done (2). Which of these determinations we make is often a function of the nature of the probability table we are using, and it may allow only option (3). Examples of these procedures are given below.

Using the Normal Distribution: Tables of standard normal probabilities are set up in various ways, so one must be certain of the manner in which the table being used is set up. The format of Table 2 is one of the more common ways in which such normal probability tables are set up. Physically, the table is set up with z-scores to one decimal place in the first column (row index), with the column headings for the remaining columns giving the hundredths value (second decimal place) for the z-score. The body of the table gives the probability associated with the given z-score, with more extreme (larger) z-scores being less probable. The table includes only the positive values for the z-scores, those from 0 to 3.0. Thus, since the standard normal distribution is symmetric about its mean of zero, probabilities for negative z-scores are read from the same table. The usual information sought in a test of significance is the probability associated

TABLE 2
Probabilities in the Upper Portion of the Standard Normal Distribution[a]

z	.00	.01	.02	.03	.04	.05	.06	.07	.08	.09
.0	.500	.496	.492	.488	.484	.480	.476	.472	.468	.464
.1	.460	.456	.452	.448	.444	.440	.436	.433	.429	.425
.2	.421	.417	.413	.409	.405	.401	.397	.394	.390	.386
.3	.382	.378	.374	.371	.367	.363	.359	.356	.352	.348
.4	.345	.341	.337	.334	.330	.326	.323	.319	.316	.312
.5	.309	.305	.302	.298	.295	.291	.288	.284	.281	.278
.6	.274	.271	.268	.264	.261	.258	.255	.251	.248	.245
.7	.242	.239	.236	.233	.230	.227	.224	.221	.218	.215
.8	.212	.209	.206	.203	.200	.198	.195	.192	.189	.187
.9	.184	.181	.179	.176	.174	.171	.169	.166	.164	.161
1.0	.159	.156	.154	.152	.149	.147	.145	.142	.140	.138
1.1	.136	.133	.131	.129	.127	.125	.123	.121	.119	.117
1.2	.115	.113	.111	.109	.107	.106	.104	.102	.100	.099
1.3	.097	.095	.093	.092	.090	.089	.087	.085	.084	.082
1.4	.081	.079	.078	.076	.075	.074	.072	.071	.069	.068
1.5	.067	.066	.064	.063	.062	.061	.059	.058	.057	.056
1.6	.055	.054	.053	.052	.051	.049	.048	.047	.046	.046
1.7	.045	.044	.043	.042	.041	.040	.039	.038	038	.037
1.8	.036	.035	.034	.034	.033	.032	.031	.031	.030	.029
1.9	.029	.028	.027	.027	.026	.026	.025	.024	.024	.023
2.0	.023	.022	.022	.021	.021	.020	.020	.019	.019	.018
2.1	.018	.017	.017	.017	.016	.016	.015	.015	.015	.014
2.2	.014	.014	.013	.013	.013	.012	.012	.012	.011	.011
2.3	.011	.010	.010	.010	.010	.009	.009	.009	.009	.008
2.4	.008	.008	.008	.008	.007	.007	.007	.007	.007	.006
2.5	.006	.006	.006	.006	.006	.005	.005	.005	.005	.005
2.6	.005	.005	.004	.004	.004	.004	.004	.004	.004	.004
2.7	.003	.003	.003	.003	.003	.003	.003	.003	.003	.003
2.8	.003	.002	.002	.002	.002	.002	.002	.002	.002	.002
2.9	.002	.002	.002	.002	.002	.002	.002	.001	.001	.001

[a]The probabilities were obtained through the use of the UNIVAC 1108 STATPAC subroutine RNORM.

with a given or more extreme z-score, and this probability can be read directly from Table 2. Tables set up in other fashions require some simple arithmetic (such as subtracting the table value from .5) to get this probability. Using Table 2, we can find the probability associated with a z-score of 1.53 by reading down the row index column to 1.5, and then across to the column headed .03 (1.5 + .03 = 1.53) to get the value .063 as the requisite probability. If we wish to know the z-score associated with a particular probability, say .025, that is, a z-score such that it and more extreme scores would occur less than 2.5% of the time, we read through the body of the table until we find .025, and read the z-score associated with it. In this case, .025 is found the column headed .06, and the row indexed 1.9. The requisite z-score is thus 1.9 + .06 = 1.96.

Using the t-Distribution: As noted previously, the t-distribution is dependent on degrees of freedom. This poses a problem in setting up tables of probabilities, since each degree of freedom considered would require a table such as the one given for the standard normal distribution. To simplify matters somewhat, tables of the t-distribution are set up so that only certain probability levels are presented, usually multiples of .05, though .025 and .01 are usually included. The values given in the body of these tables are values of t, and the associated probabilities are for the given values of t, with more extreme (larger) values being less probable. An abbreviated example of such a table is Table 3. For example, if we wish to find the t-score associated with a probability of .05, with 7 degrees of freedom, we would go to the row of the table for 7 degrees of freedom, read across to the column headed .05, and read the required t-score. In this case it is 1.90. Finding the probability of a particular t-score is a little more involved, and will only be an approximation since linear interpolation is required. Suppose we wanted the probability associated with a t-score of 1.97 and 8 degrees of freedom. The two tabled values that bracket this value are 1.86 and 2.31. These represent probabilities of .05 and .025, respectively. Our interpolation, .025 + ((1.97 − 1.86)(.05 − .025)/ (2.31 − 1.86)), gives a value of approximately .03 for the probability. Since the t-distribution is symmetric around the mean of zero, probabilities for negative scores are read from the same table. Thus, the probability associated with a score of −1.97 would still be .03. In other words, we always look up the probability of the absolute value of the score, where an absolute value is considered as the value of the number treated as a positive number. For example, the absolute value of −1.97 is 1.97.

Using the χ^2 Distribution: The nature of the probability tables for the chi-square distribution is the same as for the t-distribution. Rows of the

TABLE 3

Critical Values of *t* for Selected Probabilities in the Upper Portion of the *t*-Distribution, Selected Degrees of Freedom[a]

Degrees of Freedom	Probability			
	.10	.05	.025	.01
1	3.09	6.32	12.71	31.82
2	1.89	2.92	4.30	6.97
3	1.64	2.35	3.18	4.54
4	1.53	2.13	2.78	3.75
5	1.48	2.02	2.57	3.37
6	1.44	1.94	2.45	3.14
7	1.42	1.90	2.37	3.00
8	1.40	1.86	2.31	2.90
9	1.38	1.83	2.26	2.82
10	1.37	1.81	2.23	2.76

[a]The *t*-values and probabilities were obtained through the use of the UNIVAC 1108 STATPAC subroutine STUD, and linear interpolation.

table indicate degrees of freedom, the columns indicate probability levels, the values in the body of the table are the values of chi-square, and the probabilities given are for the given values of chi-square, with more extreme (larger) values being less probable. Table 4 gives an abbreviated version of a typical chi-square table. If we want to find a chi-square value corresponding to a probability of .05 for 6 degrees of freedom, we would

TABLE 4

Critical Values of Chi-square for Selected Probabilities in the Upper Portion of the Chi-square Distribution, Selected Degrees of Freedom[a]

Degrees of Freedom	Probability			
	.10	.05	.025	.01
1	2.71	3.84	5.02	6.66
2	4.61	6.00	7.38	9.21
3	6.25	7.82	9.35	11.35
4	7.78	9.49	11.14	13.28
5	9.24	11.07	12.83	15.09
6	10.65	12.59	14.45	16.81
7	12.02	14.07	15.01	18.48
8	13.36	15.51	17.54	20.09
9	14.68	16.92	19.02	21.67
10	15.99	18.31	20.48	23.21

[a]The Chi-square values and probabilities were obtained through use of the UNIVAC 1108 STATPAC subroutine CHI, and linear interpolation.

go to the row for 6 degrees of freedom and across to the column headed .05 (sometimes this will be indicated as .95, for the 95th percentile point when the table is for the cumulative chi-square distribution), and read the requisite chi-square value: 12.59. To find the approximate probability associated with a particular sample chi-square value, we would interpolate in the same fashion as we did with the t-distribution.

Using the F-Distribution: The nature of the F-table is much the same as the nature of the chi-square table, except that now two degrees of freedom dimensions are involved. The complications introduced by two different degrees of freedom dimensions is solved by setting up tables for a single probability level (or occasionally two probability levels) with the values in the table being the F-values, and the given level of probability being for the tabled value of F, with more extreme (larger) values of F being less probable. The tables are usually set up with the degrees of freedom for the numerator (often called the larger estimate) of the F-ratio as column headings, and the degrees of freedom for the denominator of the F-ratio (often called the smaller estimate) as row indexes or labels. Table 5 is an abbreviated F-table for the .05 probability level. If we have a calculated F-value of 5.35 for 3 and 4 degrees of freedom (3 for the numerator and 4 for the denominator), often symbolized as $F_{3,4} = 5.35$, we can determine if this result is more or less probable than the probability level used (.05), by going to the row for 4 degrees of freedom for the denominator, and across to the column for 3 degrees of freedom for

TABLE 5

Critical Values of F for the Upper Portion of the F-Distribution, .05 Probability, Selected Degrees of Freedom[a]

Denominator	Degrees of Freedom Numerator			
	1	2	3	4
1	163.76	202.55	217.75	225.37
2	18.52	19.01	19.18	19.26
3	10.13	9.55	9.28	9.12
4	7.71	6.95	6.59	6.39
5	6.61	5.79	5.41	5.19
6	5.99	5.14	4.76	4.54
7	5.59	4.74	4.35	4.12
8	5.32	4.46	4.07	3.48
9	5.12	4.26	3.86	3.63
10	4.97	4.10	3.71	3.48

[a]The F-values were obtained through the use of the UNIVAC 1108 STATPAC subroutine FISH and linear interpolation. (Due to the nature of the interpolation, critical values for 1 degree of freedom in the denominator are poor approximations of published table values.)

the numerator. The indicated F-value in the table is 6.59. Since the calculated F-value is smaller than 6.59, the calculated F is more probable than 6.59. In other words, the probability of the value 5.35 is somewhat larger than .05, though without a table for the .10 level of significance, we cannot determine the approximate probability for this value since interpolation cannot be done without the additional information.

What has been described above as ways to use probability distributions is correct for tables set up in the indicated fashion. However, tables may be set up in other, equivalent, ways—equivalent in the sense that the same probabilities or values can be found from them—so one must always be aware of the manner in which the table is set up, so that the proper arithmetic can be employed to obtain the desired information.

Logic of Hypothesis Testing

Hypothesis testing, to most of us, means testing scientific hypotheses. Hypotheses in this sense are statements involving substantive concepts, designed to either explain or predict the phenomena in question. Typically these scientific, or substantive, hypotheses state the condition under which the phenomenon is expected to occur, and how other phenomena impinge on this occurrence. In significance testing, however, what is tested is a statistical hypothesis. A statistical hypothesis is a statement about a population parameter, or parameters. Statistical hypotheses are usually not the same as the substantive, or scientific, hypotheses that we wish to test, but should be a logical consequence of the substantive hypotheses.

Substantive, or scientific, hypotheses make statements about theoretical, usually nonexistent, populations. The populations are nonexistent in the sense that they are not bound by space or time, thus all the elements of the population never exist at one time or place. Substantive hypotheses relate to a particular phenomenon as it occurred in the past, occurs in the present, and will occur in the future. Statistical hypotheses, however, refer only to existent populations, that is, populations whose elements are available for sampling purposes.

In testing a hypothesis, whether substantive or statistical, we would like to be able to conclude that it is either true or false. Unfortunately, logical considerations prevent such clear-cut positive or negative conclusions. A simple logical argument *purporting* to prove something to be true has the following form:

$$A \to B$$
$$\underline{B}$$
$$A$$

The argument starts with the premise that if A is true, then B is true. We investigate the phenomena B, and find that B is true. We then conclude that A is true. Unfortunately, the argument is fallacious, and is often referred to as the fallacy of affirming the consequent (Copi, 1953: 251). Finding B to be true does not allow us to conclude that A is true, as there may be many factors other than A which lead to B. However, it cannot be denied that given the premise and the truth of B, A becomes more credible. In effect, this means that we cannot prove a hypothesis to be true. We may find evidence that supports the hypothesis (at least is consistent with or doesn't contradict it), and thus makes it more credible, but we can never conclusively prove the hypothesis to be true.

Null Hypothesis: There is, however, an alternative form of the argument stated above that bears heavily on significance testing procedures. This argument has the following form:

$$A \to B$$
$$\frac{-B}{-A}$$

This argument starts with the same premise as above, but in this case it is found that B is false. This allows us to conclude that A is false. This form of the argument, often referred to as *modus tollens*, is valid. This means that, though we cannot prove a hypothesis to be true, we can disprove a hypothesis. It is because of the validity of the *modus tollens* form of the argument that R. A. Fisher (1925) introduced the notion of the null hypothesis and significance testing.

To summarize, we cannot prove a hypothesis to be true. From a logical point of view, the only alternatives open in a test of significance are that we can either reject a null hypothesis, or we can fail to reject the null hypothesis. The term "fail to reject" is not synonymous with "accept!" Technically speaking, it is not possible to accept a hypothesis—particularly if this implies that one considers the hypothesis to be true—as the discussion of the fallacy of affirming the consequent indicated. However, a failure to reject a hypothesis does make the hypothesis more credible. In point of fact, if one thinks about it carefully, what we consider to be scientific knowledge comes about not by proving a hypothesis to be true, but by finding that we cannot prove it false, while at the same time having eliminated competing hypotheses. Knowledge, when viewed from this perspective is problematic. What are considered to be scientific truths are simply those statements which we consider to have a low probability of being proven incorrect in the future.[11]

The term "null hypothesis" is often confusing, as it is used in at least three distinguishable, but overlapping, senses. In the sense that Fisher introduced it, "null hypothesis" meant a hypothesis complementary to (or the negation of) a research hypothesis that one believed to be true. One set up the null hypothesis specifically to be rejected, or "nullified," so that its complement, the research hypothesis, could be considered to be true. A second sense in which the term null is used is to specify a parameter of zero. The third sense in which null is used is an outgrowth of the decision theory approach to significance testing which uses the term to specify the hypothesis which is being tested, that is, the hypothesis on which the sampling distribution is based. In the decision theory approach, one is deciding between two statistical hypotheses, one of which defines the sampling distribution and is specified as the null.

An example of the first sense in which the term "null" is used would be the following. If one assumes that the incidence of juvenile delinquency is related to the incidence of broken homes, one would set up a null hypothesis that states that there is no relationship between the two phenomena. The logic of this is that if the hypothesis of no relation can be rejected, the rational conclusion has to be that there is a relationship between the phenomena.[12] In other words, one proceeds by eliminating either the null or the alternative. The hypothesis that is not eliminated is the one to be believed. The thrust of this approach is that the null hypothesis is set up to be rejected—it is not the one the researcher believes is true.

To illustrate the second sense, we could specify the hypothesis that the difference in the rate of juvenile delinquency for children from broken homes and the rate of juvenile delinquency for children from intact homes is zero. In this case the parameter is a difference (between two rates), and we are hypothesizing that this parameter is zero.

To illustrate the third sense, we could set up two hypotheses: one states that the correlation between the incidence of juvenile delinquency and the incidence of broken homes (as measured by, say, the Pearsonian correlation coefficient) is .21; the second states that the correlation is .37. If we believed the higher correlation to be the true correlation, we might pick it as our null hypothesis, though there are a number of other considerations—including the consideration of which hypothesized parameter results in the easiest to derive sampling distribution, and some philosophical issues regarding the nature of proof—which might affect our choice of one over the other as the null hypothesis.

Finally, it should be noted that the initial null hypothesis could be interpreted in all three senses, since it not only was set up as a "straw man," but also hypothesized a parameter of zero, and in conjunction with a second hypothesis (such as the correlation is .37) could be specified as the null hypothesis in the third sense, since the sampling distribution for a correlation of .00 is the simpler of the two. Thus it is not just the form and content of the hypothesis, but the manner in which it is used as well, that may be implied by the designation of null hypothesis. Thus, there is a basic difference between the Fisher approach to significance testing and the decision theory approach to significance testing that needs some elaboration, as this difference has been at the root of many misunderstandings of the purpose and the interpretation of these techniques.

Significance testing, as introduced by R. A. Fisher, had as its purpose the testing of scientific hypotheses on the basis of limited information. Essentially, a decision on the validity of a hypothesis was to be made on the basis of a single test of the hypothesis, with the possible option of suspending judgment if the results were not clear cut enough—in other words, if the null hypothesis could not be rejected. Null hypotheses were eliminated if the sample data one observed were very unlikely if the null hypothesis were true, thus lending credence to the research hypothesis. Decision theory, however, is oriented to a different type of problem, a situation in which a decision *must* be made on the basis of limited information, and can be made rationally through minimizing the costs of making a wrong decision. One of the better illustrations of the type of problem to which the application of decision theory is very useful is in quality control. In this situation one has some process in operation—say a production line—with some product resulting, widgets as example. Generally a small number of defective widgets can be tolerated, but if the proportion of defective widgets exceeds a certain amount, the loss in sales, good will, and the cost of replacements will exceed what it would cost in lost production to shut down the production line to correct for defective machinery. On the other hand, it is possible that samples from a properly functioning production line would make it look like the line was producing too many defective widgets, and shutting down the line would result in an unnecessary and costly loss of production. In a quality control situation such as this, where the amount of profit is affected by either inaction (keeping the production line running) or action (shutting down the production line for repairs), decisions must be made one way or another if profits are to be maximized. The competing hypotheses are that the production line is functioning properly, and that the production line is defective. As information from samples taken from the production line is assessed, that is, used to test these hypotheses, a decision must be made to accept one or the other and then either continue production, or shut the line down for repairs. An important ingredient, then, in the situation for which decision theory is applicable, is the neccessity for a decision to accept one or the other hypothesis, and act in accordance. A second, equally important ingredient in the situations for which decision theory is applicable, is the ability to employ a rational process to minimize losses resulting from making incorrect decisions (shutting down a properly functioning production line or failing to shut down a faulty production line) in order to maximize profits.

Unfortunately, what comes through in most teaching of statistics is a curious mixture of the Fisher approach and the decision theory approach. Hypothesis testing is taught as if tests of scientific hypotheses—on which an immediate decision is usually unnecessary, and for which one cannot assign costs to either accepting a false hypothesis or rejecting a true hypothesis—are to be conducted as though one must make a decision and can proceed to do so on a rational basis.

Statistical hypotheses will be symbolized in this paper by an H followed by a subscript o or a to signify the null or alternate hypothesis, and a statement about a parameter. For example, if we wished to specify, as our null hypothesis, that a difference between the means of two variables is zero, the hypothesis would be written as follows:

$$\text{Ho: } \mu_1 - \mu_2 = 0$$

An alternative to the null hypothesis might be written as:

$$\text{Ha: } \mu_1 - \mu_2 \neq 0.$$

The null hypothesis specified above is an example of a *point*, or *exact*, hypothesis, in that it specifies a single value for the parameter. The alternative hypothesis is an example of an *inexact hypothesis*, as it specifies a range of values for the parameter—any value other than zero.

In significance testing, we make a number of assumptions, most of which are untested or untestable. Most are made in order that the sampling distribution for the statistics of interest can be derived, thus the validity of any of the statistical inferences we make are contingent on the extent to which these assumptions are met, or the extent to which the technique is robust with respect to violations of the assumption(s).

As has been indicated earlier, the most important assumption made is that the appropriate probability sample has been obtained. Since almost all standard tests of significance require that the sampling procedure be simple random, for all practical purposes this is the sampling procedure that is assumed. Depending on the technique, other assumptions which may be made are that the populations are normally distributed, that samples are independent, that samples are correlated, that population variances are equal, and so on. In discussing techniques later, important assumptions will be noted.

Actually testing a statistical hypothesis involves a number of steps. In sequence, they are:

(1) specifying the null and alternative hypotheses,

(2) choosing the appropriate statistic,

(3) deciding what will constitute an unlikely enough value for the statistic to lead to the decision that the null hypothesis is false,

(4) calculating the statistic from a set of randomly sampled cases, and finally,

(5) deciding whether or not to reject the null hypothesis on the basis of the sample statistic.

Alternative Hypothesis: The statement of the statistical hypotheses (null and alternative) is dependent on the nature of the research hypothesis and general level of knowledge about the phenomena, as well as the technique chosen to test the hypothesis. Briefly, since these will be elaborated later, hypotheses to be tested may specify whole distributions, parameters indicating central tendency or location, parameters specifying variability, parameters specifying differences in characteristics of populations, parameters specifying either form or strength of relationship, and so on. Once the null hypothesis is specified, the nature of the alternate hypothesis is usually resolved in terms of the amount of information the researcher has about the phenomena or phenomenon under study. If the information is minimal, so that neither a directional nor exact hypothesis may be specified as the alternative, the alternative will usually be a non-directional alternative. As example, if we were testing a hypothesis about a difference in means we might specify a null and alternative as above and signify, by doing so, that all we can expect if the null hypothesis is false is that there is some difference between the means of the populations, with no basis for expecting the mean of population one to be larger or smaller than the mean of population two. However, if we happened to be dealing with weights of males and females, with population one being females and population two being males, and knowing what most of us know about males and females, we would most likely set as our alternative the inexact hypothesis that the average weight for males would be greater than the average weight for females, as follows:

$$Ha: \mu_1 - \mu_2 < 0$$

Our ability to specify a directional alternative, it must be noted, is based totally and strictly on our prior knowledge of the likely state of the phenomenon—and may be a consequence of either theory or prior empirical findings. It is improper to state a directional alternative after having looked at the data as this spuriously increases the power of the test (see the section on power below). If our knowledge of weight differentials between males and females were detailed enough, we might specify our alternative more precisely as a point or exact hypothesis as follows:

$$Ha: \mu_1 - \mu_2 = 12.5$$

In this instance, we would then be deciding between two point, or exact, hypotheses. However, other than the trivial null hypothesis specifying a parameter of zero, point or exact hypotheses are virtually nonexistent in social research, and thus discussions of such hypotheses are of little value other than as pedagogical devices for explaining certain statistical concepts.

Level of Significance: Earlier it was indicated that in significance testing, what we do is compare the sample statistic with the hypothesized parameter in the light of the amount of variation which can be expected on the basis of chance factors. The sampling distribution indicates the amount and "pattern" of variation expected on the basis of chance.

The test of significance will provide us with information to make a decision between two possible situations:

(1) the sample statistic is close enough to the value hypothesized that the difference between the two is considered to be due to chance factors in the sampling process, and we will have no grounds for doubting the null hypothesis, or

(2) the difference between the sample statistic and the hypothesized parameter is so great that we will no longer attribute the difference to sampling error, but will attribute the difference to the null hypothesis being false.

This still does not determine for us what will be considered too great a difference to be attributed to chance fluctuations in sampling, and unfortunately there is no mathematical or other theory which will do this for us. The decision as to what is too unlikely to be attributed to sampling error, for all practical purposes is *totally arbitrary,* though certain conventions have been adopted by researchers to "standardize" procedures. However, to use conventional standards for a definition of what differences can be attributed to chance fluctuations in samples when the hypothesis is in fact true, is simply to camouflage the arbitrariness of the standard. The choice, whether determined with or without considerations of convention, is still an arbitrary choice.

The definition of a difference too large to be attributable to chance fluctuations in sampling (sampling error) will, in significance testing, always be in terms of a *probability*. Evidence that the null hypothesis is false is in the form of a statistic which would occur with a probability that is equal to, or smaller than, a previously set probability that was decided upon as indicating a result too unlikely to occur if the null hypothesis were true. The probability that is used to indicate too unlikely a statistic for us to fail to reject the null is called the *level of significance* (or significance level). Thus we might take .05 as the level of significance, meaning that any statistic which would occur with a probability of .05 or less if the null hypothesis were true will be considered sufficient evidence to consider the null hypothesis false. Often the significance level is stated in terms of a percentage rather than a proportion. Thus equivalently, we may speak of the .05 level, or the 5% level of significance.

Once we have set this probability (level of significance) we have some equivalent procedural options, depending on the statistic which we are using, the available tables of sampling distributions, and our predilections. One option is to calculate directly the probability of our sample statistic, and to compare this probability with our level of significance. (This will often be our procedure if we are dealing with a statistic whose sampling distribution is the binomial distribution.) A second option is to calculate a test statistic, such as a z-score from our sample statistic, and from the table giving the sampling distribution of the statistic, determine the probability for our sample statistic and base our decision on whether or not the probability does, or does not, exceed the significance level. A third option is to set our level of significance, go to the table for our test statistic and find the value of that statistic that occurs with the probability indicated in the significance level, and use that value as a *critical value* against which we will compare the test statistic we calculate from our sample. The critical value defines an area, beginning at the critical value and extending over values of the sample statistic that are less probable, that is called the *region of rejection*, or the *critical region*. If the test statistic falls into the region of rejection, the null hypothesis is rejected. As indicated, in terms of making a decision, these are equivalent procedures, and they will always result in the same decision for a given sample statistic. Illustrations will be provided later to demonstrate the equivalence.

Region of Rejection (Critical Region) Placement: The null hypothesis is rejected when two conditions hold simultaneously:

(1) the sample statistic is *un*likely if the null hypothesis is true, *and*

(2) the sample statistic is likely if the alternative hypothesis is true.

The critical value(s) and region(s) of rejection must be placed so that both criteria are met simultaneously.

The first condition is met whenever the sample result (test statistic) differs sufficiently from the expected value of the sampling distribution (which is based on the null hypothesis) in either direction—smaller than the expected value or larger than the expected value.

The second condition is met when the sample result is in the direction(s) "predicted" by the alternative hypothesis. If the alternative is nondirectional, a result in either direction from the expected value of the sampling distribution is consistent with the alternative hypothesis, so a region of rejection is placed in both tails of the sampling distribution. This situation is usually called a *two-tailed test*. More specifically, one-half of the area representing the level of significance is placed in each tail of the sampling distribution. Thus, for a .05 significance level, .025 of the area is placed in each tail. This procedure is always followed when the sampling distribution is either the normal or t-distribution, but *not necessarily when the normal distribution is used as an approximation* to the actual sampling distribution of the test statistic.[13] If the alternative is directional, all of the area represented by the level of significance, that is, the region of rejection, is placed in the tail predicted by the alternative. This situation is usually referred to as a *one-tailed test*. For example, in the illustration earlier of a test of a hypothesis about the difference between the weights of males and females, the directional alternative hypothesis specified that the average weight of males would be greater than the average weight of females, so—as long as the test statistic is based on subtracting the male average weight from the female average weight, giving a negative value for the expected difference—this would lead us to place the region of rejection in the tail of the sampling distribution representing negative (smaller than zero) values of the test statistic. (When the null hypothesis specifies no difference in the average weights, the expected value for the sampling distribution will be zero.)

The logic underlying the placement of regions of rejection as indicated above is simple and straightforward when the sampling distribution is the normal or t-distribution. Unfortunately, the logic of region of rejection placement based on the nature of the alternative hypothesis breaks down in most applications of the chi-square and F-distributions. In most of the situations in which the F- or chi-square distributions are used as the sampling distribution, even when the alternative hypothesis is nondirectional, the region of rejection will be set up *as though the alternative hypothesis is directional.* This situation, also, is commonly referred to as a *one-tailed test.* The logic for treating most aplications of the *F*- and chi-square distributions as though the alternative hypothesis were directional is related to the fact that if the null hypothesis is false the values of *F* and chi-square can only be larger than the expected values of the *F*- and chi-square distributions. However, these two different bases for one-tailed tests can be a source of confusion, so one has to look at the nature of the test statistic as well as the alternative hypothesis in determining region of rejection placement.

Equivalences Among Sampling Distributions: Though we will not go into the mathematics of the equivalences, only state them, there are several mathematical equivalances among the four sampling distributions we have discussed. These are:

(1) A *z*-score is equivalent to the square root of a chi-square with one degree of freedom.

(2) An *F* with one and *N* degrees of freedom is equal to the square of a *t*-score with *N* degrees of freedom.

(3) A *t*-score with degrees of freedom greater than about 120 is approximately equal to a *z*-score.

Symbolically these relations are:

$$z \quad = (\chi_1^2)^{\frac{1}{2}}$$

$$t_N^2 \quad = F_{1,N}$$

$$t_{120} \cong z.$$

By saying that the equivalences are mathematical equivalences, we mean only that algebraic substitution of appropriate quantities into the formulas for the quantities on the left side of the above equations results in the formulas for the quantities on the right side of the equations or vice versa. Unfortunately, the various equivalent values represented, except the equivalence between the *t*- and *z*-distributions, will *not* cut off the equivalent proportion of the sampling distributions! For example, a chi-square of 3.84 with one degree of freedom cuts off .05 of the tail of the chi-square distribution. The square root of 3.84 gives a value of 1.96 (within rounding error), which cuts off .025 of the tail of the normal distribution. Similarly, a *t*-score of 4.30 with two degrees of freedom cuts off .025 of the tail of the distribution. The square of this value is 18.49, which is (within rounding error) the F-value for one and two degrees of freedom which cuts off .05 of the tail of the F-distribution. If such comparisons were to be systematically carried out for all the appropriate z- and chi-square values, and all the appropriate t- and F-values it would be found that the relation between the significance levels is that if the chi-square values were significant at the α level, the z-values would be significant at the ½ α level. Similarly, for F-values significant at the α level, the equivalent t-values would be significant at the ½ α level.

Types of Error, Power: The logic of tests of significance guarantees that some of the decisions we make about a null hypothesis will be wrong. A moment's reflection should indicate why this is the case. Remember that a sampling distribution reflects all the possible values that can result for the sample or test statistic simply on the basis of sampling error. Yet, we arbitrarily designate some of these values (those in the region of rejection) as evidence that the null hypothesis is false. This means that the logic of tests of significance guarantees that in the long run we will reject a true null hypothesis the proportion of times we have set as the significance level. The incorrect rejection of a true null hypothesis is called a Type I error, or alpha (α) error, and the probability of a Type I error is equal to the level of significance. There is yet another error which we can make. That error is in failing to reject a false null hypothesis. This error is called a Type II or beta (β) error.[14] Again, it should be noted that these errors are a result of the logic of significance testing, and cannot be avoided. The two types of errors are related in that minimizing the probability of a Type I error increases the probability of making a Type II error.

The *power of a test* is defined as $1-\beta$, that is, 1 minus the probability of a Type II error, and is the probability of rejecting a false null hypothesis. In order to calculate β, the alternative hypothesis must be an exact hypothesis.[15] Since it is extremely rare in social science that one has an exact hypothesis specified as the alternative hypothesis, it is rare that the power of the test is calculated.

4. TESTS OF SIGNIFICANCE

The significance tests employed in the following sections have been chosen because they illustrate many of the basic ideas in significance testing, and make use of the more commonly employed theoretical sampling distributions. The examples used are hypothetical (hypothetical data) but within the range of real data.

Comparing Whole Distributions—Goodness of Fit

Suppose we had a pair of dice that we thought were fair, but we decided to run a test to see if it was reasonable to continue in this belief. From Figure 1 we get the theoretical distribution which should be approximated by a sample of rolls of our pair of dice. Suppose we roll the dice 180 times and record the results (Table 6). The expected number of times each total should occur is obtained by taking the total number of rolls and multiplying by the theoretical proportion (Np_i). Thus, on the average in 180 rolls of a pair of fair dice we would expect about 5 times we would get a sum (score) of 2, about 25 times, on the average, we would get a sum (score) of 6, and so on. How close are these actual and expected distributions? Following convention in significance testing, we will say that any deviation from the expected distribution that would occur less than 5% of the time (5%, or .05, level of significance) on the basis of sampling—that is, our 180 rolls of the dice—will be evidence that our null hypothesis (that the dice are fair) is false. (An alternative way of stating the null hypothesis is that we have sampled from the distribution specified by the "expected" column.) The alternative hypothesis is that we have sampled from a population that differs from the theoretical in some unspecified manner.

Chi-Square Tests: The statistic χ^2 (Pearson's chi-square, or simply chi-square), which has a sampling distribution that is approximated by the theoretical chi-square distribution, can be used to compare sample distributions with hypothesized population distributions. The formula is:

TABLE 6
Hypothetical Data, 180 Rolls of a Pair of Dice

Score	Theoretical Proportion	Expected Occurences	Actual Occurences
2	1/36	5	7
3	2/36	10	9
4	3/36	15	18
5	4/36	20	20
6	5/36	25	35
7	6/36	30	30
8	5/36	25	23
9	4/36	20	20
10	3/36	15	10
11	2/36	10	5
12	1/36	5	3
	36/36	180	180

$$\chi^2_{k-1} = \Sigma(f_o - f_e)^2/f_e$$

where $k-1$ is the degrees of freedom,[16] f_o represents the frequencies from our sample, f_e represents the expected frequencies and k is the number of categories in the theoretical distribution. The χ^2 calculations for the data in Table 6 are given in Table 7. What values of χ^2 lead to a rejection of the null hypothesis? From a quick glance at the formula, it is apparent that χ^2 will be zero if the sample distribution exactly matches the hypothesized distribution (population distribution), and that as the difference between the two distributions gets larger and larger, the value of χ^2 gets larger and larger. Thus, evidence against the null hypothesis and for the alternative is in the form of large values of χ^2.

How much variation can we expect on the basis of sampling error? In other words, how big a difference can we attribute to the vagaries of sampling error? We have already indicated by the choice of a level of significance that we will reject the null hypothesis any time the test statistic (χ^2) is so large that it would occur 5% or less of the time if the null hypothesis were in fact true. (Notice that we don't really specify a difference, all we specify is a probability, and the sampling distribution lets us know if the difference between what we observed and what we expected is too large to be attributed to sampling error.) To determine whether or not the results we obtained could be attributed to sampling error rather than to the null hypothesis being false, we have to compare our results with the critical value found in the sampling distribution, the theoretical chi-square distribution (see Table 4). The critical value for the 5% level of significance and 10 degrees of freedom is 18.31. (Some tables will provide

TABLE 7
Calculations for Hypothetical Data on 180 Rolls of a Pair of Dice

f_o	f_e	f_o-f_e	$(f_o-f_e)^2$	$(f_o-f_e)^2/f_e$
7	5	2	4	.8
9	10	1	1	.1
18	15	3	9	.6
20	20	0	0	.0
35	25	10	100	4.0
30	30	0	0	.0
23	25	2	4	.16
20	20	0	0	.0
10	15	5	25	1.67
5	10	5	25	2.5
3	5	2	4	.8
180	180			10.63

values with different numbers of significant digits, so don't be concerned if a table you are using gives the critical value as 18.3, or 18.307, or even some more precise quantity.) This means that we would have to obtain a χ^2 value of 18.3 or larger in order to reject the null hypothesis. Since our calculated value is 10.63, we fail to reject the null hypothesis. On this basis it would be reasonable for us to continue to believe we have a pair of dice that are fair, but by no means have we proven that the dice are fair. Our evidence is simply consistent with the hypothesis, nothing more.

If we are interested in determining how likely our particular result is, assuming the null hypothesis is true, we could look along the row representing the degrees of freedom for our test, 10 degrees of freedom, until we found either our calculated χ^2 value (which is very unlikely, since only selected values, usually corresponding to probabilities that are multiples of .05, are presented), or two values such that our calculated value falls between them. (This requires the use of a more complete table than the abbreviated chi-square table presented as Table 4 in this paper.) Then by simple interpolation, we can usually get a reasonable estimate of the probability of our result. In our case the calculated value of 10.63 lies approximately .6 of the way between 12.5, the critical value for a 50% level of significance, and 9.3, the critical value for a 25% level of significance. Thus the calculated value of 10.63 is significant at approximately the 40% level of significance. Put another way, about 40% of the time, in the long run, we would expect to get greater deviations from the expected distribution if the null hypothesis were true.

As another example of a goodness of fit test, suppose we wished to determine if the pattern of memberships in social organizations is the same in urban communities as was earlier found in a rural community (Kaufman, 1944). The theoretical distribution on which the expected frequencies are based is given in the first column of Table 8, and is the proportion distribution obtained in Kaufman's study. To test the hypothesis that the patterns of membership are the same, we set up the null hypothesis that we have sampled from the population specified by the theoretical distribution (an equivalent way of stating the null is that there is no difference between the rural and urban populations with respect to patterns of membership) and we have drawn a simple random sample of 300 cases from our urban community. The results of the sample are given in the last column of Table 8. The calculated value of chi-square for this data is 12.92. If we test the hypothesis at the .05 level, the critical value of chi-square is 7.82 (see Table 4). Thus, since our calculated value is larger than the critical value, we reject the null hypothesis, and conclude that the pattern of membership in social organizations is different in the two urban and rural communities studied. (Had we tested the hypothesis at the .01

TABLE 8

Theoretical and Actual Distributions of Memberships in Social Organizations in Rural and Urban Communities

Number of Memberships	Theoretical (Rural) Distribution	Expected Distribution	Sample (Urban) Distribution
None	.36	108	90
1-2	.40	120	150
3-4	.17	51	45
5 or more	.07	21	15
	1.00	300	300

level, the result would have been the same, as the critical value for the .01 level is 11.35, which is smaller than the obtained chi-square.)

In order to employ this chi-square goodness of fit test, in addition to the assumption of simple random sampling, we require that observations are independent, that each observation fall into only one category, and that the sample is large. Simple random sampling guarantees that the observations (values) are independent, but care must be taken that the categorization is mutually exclusive and exhaustive, so that no observation falls into more than one category. How large a sample is needed is open to debate, but a partial answer can be given in terms of expected frequencies. For 1 degree of freedom the minimum expected frequency should be 10 or more. For 2 or more degrees of freedom, the minimum expected frequency should be 5 or more. Thus, one should draw samples that are large enough to meet these minimal criteria. The requirement for expected values of a certain size is due to the fact that in developing the sampling distribution for χ^2 it is necessary to assume that observed values are normally distributed around the expected value. Small expected values lead to a violation of this since the distribution of observed values around small expected frequencies will be strongly skewed.

To get around the problem with small expected frequencies after one has drawn a sample, it is often suggested that categories be combined in such a way that expected frequencies are of the proper size. Such procedures, however, are suspect as they effectively change the nature of the sampling process so that it is no longer truly a simple random sample, and this means that the sampling distribution is affected in some unspecified manner (Hays, 1973: 736). Furthermore, after an empirical study (a Monte Carlo computer simulation), Knetz (1963) concluded that rather gross violations of the expected frequency criteria resulted in small errors.

Thus it appears more prudent to settle for probability estimates that may be incorrect, but within a percentage or so from the correct value, rather than employ a combining operation with unknown effects on the sampling distribution.

Kolmogorov-Smirnov Test: If our data are at least ordinal (we can distinguish on the basis of greater than, equal to, or less than, but do not have a unit of measurement) there is another goodness of fit test we might employ. This one is called the Kolmogorov-Smirnov one-sample test. The logic underlying this test is that if the sample comes from the population specified, the cumulative distribution for the sample ought to be very similar to the cumulative distribution for the hypothesized population. If we are testing the null hypothesis against a nondirectional alternative, the largest difference between the proportions in the two cumulative distributions must be greater than $k(1/N^{1/2})$: for the .01 level of significance $k = 1.52$, and for the .05 level of significance $k = 1.22$.[17] The test statistic is the largest difference, in absolute value, between the sample cumulative distribution (reduced to proportions) and the cumulative proportion distribution for the population. The cumulative proportions for the Kolmogorov-Smirnov test for the data in Table 6 are given in Table 9. The largest difference is .0778. In order for this to be statistically significant at the .05 level, it would have to be larger than $1.22(1/\sqrt{180})$ which is .091. Since the largest difference does not exceed this value, we would again fail to reject the null hypothesis.

TABLE 9

Cumulative Proportion Distributions for the Hypothetical Distribution of Values for 180 Rolls of a Pair of Dice

Score	Cumulative Proportion Theoretical	Sample	Difference
2	.0277	.0388	
3	.0833	.0888	
4	.1666	.1888	
5	.2777	.3000	
6	.4166	.4944	.0778
7	.5833	.6611	
8	.7222	.7888	
9	.8333	.9000	
10	.9166	.9555	
11	.9722	.9833	
12	1.0000	1.0000	

Since the number of memberships in social organizations is an ordered set of categories (ordinal) it would be proper to use the Kolmogorov-Smirnov goodness of fit test on the data in Table 8. For these data, the maximum difference between cumulative proportion differences is .06, and the value that must be exceeded for significance is $1.22(1/\sqrt{300})$ which is .070. Since the test statistic (.06) is smaller than the critical values, we would fail to reject the null hypothesis. This result is opposite of the result using the chi-square goodness of fit test on the same data. The reasons for this difference are not clear, but such differences in the results of two tests of significance pose problems for the conscientious researcher. Which of the two results is to be accepted? Unfortunately, the answer to the question is not at all clear. The major consideration in choosing between two tests should be in terms of their relative power. Yet it is not always possible to determine the power of tests in a particular application, or to generalize about the relative powers of two tests in varying circumstances. For example, when one test makes stronger assumptions than another (higher level of measurement, normal population distribution, and so on), the test requiring the stronger assumptions is usually assumed to be the more powerful. However, the assumption proves false in this comparison of the chi-square and Kolmogorov-Smirnov tests, as the Kolmogorov-Smirnov turns out to be the less powerful of the two. Thus idiosyncratic factors associated with the situation must be considered in explaining differences in power—grouping effects, sample size, pattern of differences between theoretical (expected) and actual distributions,[18] and so on. The situation for descriptive statistics is somewhat clearer. Here, in general, it pays to employ techniques which make stronger assumptions, as long as the data meet the stronger assumptions, since all the information in the data is utilized. A problem which often arises, however, is that the significance of a particular descriptive statistic is assessed by a test of significance requiring weaker assumptions than the descriptive technique used. Commonly, tests of significance requiring only nominal data, such as chi-square, are used to test the significance of descriptive statistics, such as Gamma, requiring ordinal data. In general, such situations should be avoided, as the power of the appropriate significance test for the descriptive statistic may be different from the power of the significance test actually used, and the two techniques may tap different aspects of the data. As a result, one may be misled by the results of the test.

Binomial Test: Earlier a question was raised about whether or not one could reject the hypothesis that one had a fair coin if in 20 tosses the coin turned up heads 14 times. The theoretical sampling distribution that fits this type of problem is the binomial distribution. This distribution can be used when there are only two possible outcomes of a trial (or values of a variable). Usually these outcomes are labeled success and failure. In applying the binomial, we are interested in the number of successes out of a given number of trials.

Since we are testing the hypothesis that our coin is fair, our null hypothesis is Ho: $p = .5$, where p indicates the probability of a success (in other words, if the coin is fair the probability of a head is .5). Since there is no expectation that the coin is biased in any particular fashion, the alternative hypothesis is nondirectional, and is Ha: $p \neq .5$.

If the null hypothesis is true, we would expect on the average in the long run to get heads half the time, and tails the other half of the time. Thus the outcome of the experiment that would lead to a rejection of the null hypothesis is one which differs greatly from the expectation in either direction—either a large or small number of heads. The former might lead us to suspect that $p > .5$, while the latter might lead us to suspect that $p < .5$. Since either a small or large number of heads will lead to a rejection of the null hypothesis, *both* tails of the distribution need to be considered in determining the probability of the result of our experiment. This will involve determining the probability of a *deviation from the expected value* (half heads, or 10 heads in 20 tosses) *as large or larger than we obtained in the experiment in both directions from the expected value.* Thus we will be figuring the probability of getting 14 or more heads (four more than expected), and 6 or fewer heads (four less than expected).

Though there are tables of the binomial distribution available, it is unlikely that one would have convenient access to them. This is due partly to the amount of space required—the distribution changes for each change in p and N, thus an infinite number of tables could be prepared—and to the fact that for large values of N and values of p reasonably near .5 there is a simple approximation to the binomial that is precise enough for most tests of significance. Thus, for most problems we will have to calculate the required binomial distribution, or the needed portions of it.

The theoretical binomial distribution is obtained by expanding the expression $(p + q)^N$, where N is the number of trials, p is the probability of success, q is the probability of failure, and $p + q = 1$. The probability of exactly r successes in the N trials is

$$C_{N,r}p^r q^{N-r}$$

where $C_{N,r}$ is the symbol for the number of combinations of N things taken r at a time. The formula for the number of combinations is

$$C_{N,r} = N!/(N-r)!r!$$

where the symbol "!" means factorial, and N! is

$$N! = N(N-1)(N-2)(N-3) \ldots (3)(2)(1),$$

in other words, the product of the integers 1 through N. Since the theoretical binomial distribution is a probability distribution, the terms sum to one:

$$\Sigma C_{N,r} p^r q^{N-r} = 1.$$

Thus, the distribtion we need for our problem can be obtained by solving for each of the 21 possible numbers of successes—0, 1, 2, 3, . . . , 19, 20. The resulting distribution is found in Table 10, but illustrative calculations are given below. For example, the probability of no (zero) successes in 20 trials is given by

$$(C_{20,0})(.5^0)(.5^{20-0}) = (20!/(20-0)!0!).5^{20} = .000000953674$$

For those whose algebra is a bit rusty—zero factorial (0!) is, by definition, equal to 1, and because of rules governing exponents $(b^x b^y = b^{x+y})$, the product of .5 raised to two different powers is $(.5^0)(.5^{20-0}) = .5^{20}$. Similarly, the probability of eight successes is

$$(C_{20,8})(.5^8)(.5^{20-8}) = (20!/(20-8)!8!).5^{20} = .1201343.$$

The probability of 14 or more successes is obtained from Table 10 by adding the separate probabilities of 14 successes, 15 successes, 16 successes, through 20 successes, and that probability—to four decimal places—is .0577. (Since the cumulative probabilities are also given, we could find the probability of 14 or more successes by subtracting the probability of 13 or fewer successes from 1 to get the same result, namely $1 - .9423 = .0577$.) We have not yet obtained the probability of a result as extreme in either direction as 14 heads. Since our results are 4 more heads than expected, the extreme in the opposite direction, 4 less heads than expected, is 6 or fewer heads. The probability of 6 or fewer heads can be read directly from the cumulative distribution, and is .0577. Thus the probability of a result as extreme as 14 heads is the sum of these two probabilities, or .1154. Since the level of significance chosen for our test was the .05 level, we would reject the null hypothesis if the probability of our result was less than .05, that is, between .00 and .05. Our result, .1154, is greater than .05, and thus we would accept it as resulting from chance factors when p

TABLE 10

Theoretical Binominal Distribution for N = 20, p = .5

r	P(r)	Cumulative Probability
0	$.9537 \times 10^{-6}$	.0000
1	$.1907 \times 10^{-4}$	.0000
2	$.1811 \times 10^{-3}$	.0002
3	$.1087 \times 10^{-2}$	.0013
4	$.4621 \times 10^{-2}$	.0059
5	$.1478 \times 10^{-1}$	.0207
6	$.3696 \times 10^{-1}$	.0577
7	$.7392 \times 10^{-1}$	.1316
8	.1201	.2517
9	.1602	.4119
10	.1762	.5881
11	.1602	.7483
12	.1201	.8684
13	$.7392 \times 10^{-1}$	.9423
14	$.3696 \times 10^{-1}$	.9793
15	$.1478 \times 10^{-1}$	.9941
16	$.4621 \times 10^{-2}$	.9987
17	$.1087 \times 10^{-2}$	.9998
18	$.1811 \times 10^{-3}$	.9999
19	$.1907 \times 10^{-4}$	.9999
20	$.9537 \times 10^{-6}$	1.0000

is .5. In other words, we fail to reject the null hypothesis. Put yet another way, this result (14 heads) is consistent with the hypothesis that $p = .5$, though it *does not prove* that p is .5.

The notion of the power of a test can be illustrated here. Suppose, instead of the nondirectional alternative hypothesis we used above, we had reason to suspect the coin was not fair, and more specifically, that the probability of a head was actually .7 ($p = .7$) rather than .5 ($p = .5$). The theoretical probability distribution under the hypothesis that $p = .7$ is given by Table 11. Combining the information in Tables 10 and 11 allows us to determine the probability of rejecting the null hypothesis that $p = .5$ against the alternative that $p = .7$. Figure 5 shows schematically how this is done. The distribution at the left in Figure 5 is the theoretical distribution for $p = .5$, and the distribution on the right is the theoretical distribution for $p = .7$. If the level of significance is set at .05, given the null hypothesis that $p = .5$, the critical region is the portion of the distribution representing 15 through 20 heads, as these areas sum to less than .05,

TABLE 11
Theoretical Binominal Distribution for N = 20, p = .7

r	P(r)
0	$.3487 \times 10^{-8}$
1	$.1627 \times 10^{-7}$
2	$.3607 \times 10^{-7}$
3	$.4747 \times 10^{-6}$
4	$.5008 \times 10^{-5}$
5	$.3739 \times 10^{-4}$
6	.0002
7	.0010
8	.0039
9	.0120
10	.0308
11	.0654
12	.1144
13	.1642
14	.1916
15	.1788
16	.1304
17	.0716
18	.0278
19	.0068
20	.0008
	1.0000

while including the area for 14 heads would sum to more than .05. The probability of making a Type II error is the area in the distribution for $p = .7$ for 0 through 14 heads, since these are outcomes which lead to a failure to reject the null hypothesis, and we want the probability for the situation where the alternative is actually true. In other words, if $p = .7$ is actually true, we want the probability of 14 or fewer heads. From Table 11, this probability is .5838. Since the power of a test is $1 - \beta$ (1 minus the probability of a Type II error), the power of the test is .4162. In other words, if we were testing the null hypothesis that the coin is fair against a true situation where the probability of a head is actually .7 at the .05 level, our probability of detecting the fact that the null hypothesis is false is only approximately .42, or about 4 chances out of 10.

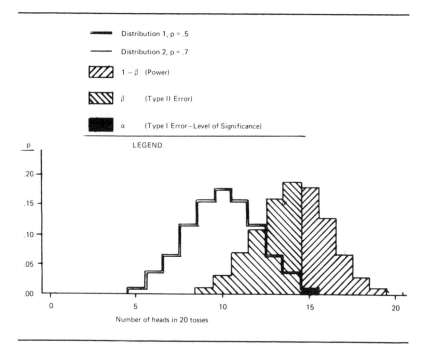

Figure 5: Type I, Type II Errors, and Power of Test Illustrated for Probability Distributions Based on the Hypotheses that p = .5, and that p = .7 for 20 Tosses of a Coin

Interestingly enough, if we had decided to test the null hypothesis at the .06 level of significance instead of the .05 level, the power of the test would have been .6078, or our chances of detecting the fact that the null hypothesis is false would have been about 6 out of 10 for an increase in power of 50%! The calculations for power if the level of significance is .06 are to find the probability of a Type II error by adding the probabilities for 0 through 13 heads for the distribution where $p = .7$ to get .3922, and then subtracting .3922 from 1 to get the power. The fact that shifting the level of significance 1% gives a 50% increase in power should give the reader pause for thought regarding the choice of levels of significance in the absence of knowledge about the power of the test.

If you have attempted to go through the complete set of calculations needed to obtain the theoretical binomial distribution in Table 10, it should be very apparent that obtaining such distributions becomes very tedious once N becomes of any size, and this is further aggravated when p is some value other than .5, as this requires raising two decimal values (both p and q) to some power. Fortunately, an approximation to the binomial distribution is available for a fairly wide range of situations. So long as N is large, and p is neither very small (close to zero) nor very large (close to one), the normal distribution can be used to approximate the binomial. Though there are no hard and fast rules as to how small or how large p must be before the approximation is too imprecise to use, or what the value of N must be to offset smaller or larger values of p, one general guide is that the smaller of either Np or Nq should be at least 5.

For appropriate situations, the transformation from the binomial to the normal is the following

$$z = [(r_p \pm .5) - E(r_p)]/\sigma_{r_p}$$

where

$$E(r_p) = Np \quad \text{and} \quad \sigma_{r_p} = (Npq)^{\frac{1}{2}}.$$

In other words, the expected number of successes for a given probability of success is the number of trials multiplied by the probability of success, and the standard deviation (standard error) is the square root of the product of the probability of success, probability of failure, and number of trials. The .5 in the numerator is a correction for continuity. It is a means of making the approximation more precise, and stems from the fact that the binomial is a discrete distribution, and the normal is a continuous distribution. A consideration of Figure 6 will help explain the purpose of the correction. First note that the histogram for the binomial distribution represents probability by the area in the rectangles representing each of the possible numbers of successes. Note also that the values representing the number of successes—0, 1, 2, and so on—are the midpoints of the bases of each of the rectangles, and that the true limits of each of the intervals representing the number of success are .5 of a unit below and above the midpoint. Thus the interval representing 5 successes extends from 4.5 to 5.5, and the probability of 5 or more successes would be found by adding the areas in the two rectangles representing 5 and 6 success. Putting it another way, the probability of 5 or more successes is the area to the right of the point 4.5 in the histogram representing the binomial distribution. If we approximate this area by using the normal distribution, and find the area beyond the value 5, we ignore the area between 4.5 and 5. To correct for this omission we subtract .5 from 5 as part of the calculation so that the area approximated is the area from 4.5 and beyond. As a general rule, the procedure in applying the correction is the following. So long as the

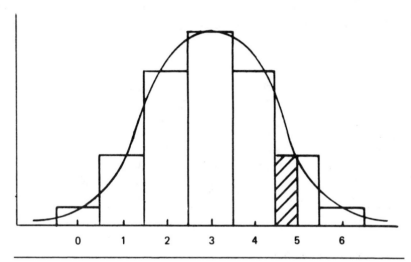

Portion of the binomial probability distribution excluded if the correction for continuity is not made when approximating the probability of five or more successes.

Figure 6: Illustration of the Correction for Continuity in the Normal Approximation to the Binomial for N = 6 and p = .5

area we are seeking to approximate is in the tail of the distribution (so that we are finding the probability of a given or more extreme number of successes), the .5 is subtracted when the number of successes is greater than the expected number of successes (that is, greater than Np), and added when the number of successes is less than the expected number of successes.[19]

Proceeding with the normal approximation for our problem, we can employ either of the procedures indicated earlier:

(1) we can calculate our test statistic, find the probability associated with it, and base our decision on that probability much as was done with the binomial above, or

(2) we can go to the table of normal distribution probabilities, and obtain the critical value for our level of significance, and then compare our calculated test statistic with the critical value and make our decision without ever determining the probability of our particular result.

For illustrative purposes, we will employ both procedures, beginning with (1).

Since we want the probability associated with an outcome as extreme as 14 or more successes, our transformation is

$$z = [(14 - .5) - 20(.5)]/2.24 = 1.565.$$

Turning now to the table of normal distribution probabilities (Table 2), we find that the area (probability) beyond the standard score (z) of 1.565 is .0588 (by interpolation between the probabilities for z values of 1.56 and 1.57). By a similar process we find the probability of 6 or fewer successes.

$$z = [(6 + .5) - 20(.5)]/12.24 = -1.565.$$

Since the normal distribution is symmetric, the area to the left of -1.565 is also .0588. Thus the probability of a result as extreme as that obtained is the sum of these two probabilities, .1176. Again, this result indicates that chance factors could have produced this result if p is .5; thus our result is again judged as being consistent with the null hypothesis. In other words, we fail to reject the null hypothesis. The decision is the same as the earlier decision based on the binomial, and the difference between the exact binomial and the normal approximation to the binomial in obtained probabilities, .0022, is so small as to be ignored. The ease in making use of the approximation more than compensates for such a minor error.

To illustrate the alternative procedure—setting a critical value—we look up in the table of normal distribution probabilities (Table 2) the z-score (standard score or standardized normal deviate) that corresponds to the previously selected .05 level of significance. Since the alternative hypothesis is nondirectional, the critical value (z-score) selected will have .025 of the area in the distribution beyond it and there will be a critical value and region of rejection in each tail. The z-score which has .025 of the area in the distribution beyond it is 1.96 in the right end of the distribution and -1.96 in the left end of the distribution. Thus any value for our test statistic greater in absolute value than the critical value of 1.96 will lead to rejection of the null hypothesis. Since we have already calculated the z-score for our experiment (-1.565), we need only compare it with 1.96 to decide that we fail to reject the null hypothesis, as the calculated z-score is considerably smaller (thus more probable, or more likely) than the critical value.

Often prior research establishes an estimate of some population parameter, such as the proportion of eligible voters who are likely to not vote in a given type of election. For example, 26% of a sample of those eligible to vote in the presidential election of 1952 failed to vote. We can use the binomial sampling distribution to determine whether or not the probability of not voting was the same in the last presidential election. (The binomial is appropriate since there are only two outcomes for any case, voting or not voting.) To test this hypothesis, we set up the null hypothesis that $p = .26$, set up the alternative hypothesis that p is some value other than .26, draw a simple random sample of 500 cases from the population of voters eligible to vote in the last presidential election, and find that 146 of the cases were nonvoters. Since N is large and p is not .5, the simplest procedure for testing the hypothesis is to use the normal approximation. The calculation is

$$z = [(146 - .5) - 500(.26)] / [500(.26)(.74)]^{\frac{1}{2}}$$

$$= 1.58.$$

For the customary .05 level of significance, testing against a nondirectional hypothesis, the critical value for the test statistic is ± 1.96. Since the test statistic is smaller than the critical value, we fail to reject the null hypothesis, and thus conclude that it is reasonable to believe that the proportion not voting in the last election is the same as at the earlier time. However, to emphasize an earlier point, this result in no way proves that the parameter is .26 (that the population proportion of nonvoters is .26); it is only consistent with such a hypothesis.

Central Tendency

Quite often a researcher is concerned with testing hypotheses about the central tendency of a distribution—usually about the mean of the distribution. Depending on the circumstances, either of two sampling distributions may be used when testing hypotheses about the mean of the distribution. These are the Student's t, or t-distribution, and the normal, or standard normal, distribution. Generally, if two assumptions are met— the population sampled is normally distributed and the population standard deviation is known—the appropriate sampling distribution is the normal distribution. The appropriate test statistic in this case is[20]

$$z = (\bar{X} - \mu)/\sigma_{\bar{X}}$$

where $\sigma_{\bar{X}} = \sigma_X / N^{\frac{1}{2}}$.

However, there are problems in making these assumptions, and the inability to meet the assumptions affects the procedures. First, if we do not know the population standard deviation, but can assume that the population is normal, we can use the standard deviation from the sample as an estimate of the population standard deviation. However, if we do so, the proper sampling distribution for the sample mean is no longer the normal, but is instead the t-distribution. The appropriate test statistic now is

$$t = (\overline{X} - \mu)/S_{\overline{x}}$$

where $S_{\overline{x}} = S_x/N^{\frac{1}{2}}$ and S_x is the estimate of σ_x obtained from the sample. In other words, the S indicates an estimate rather than the population parameter.[21] The reason that the t-distribution is appropriate in this situation is that the variance of the t-distribution is greater than the normal in cases where the number of degrees of freedom is small (that is, there is more area in the tails of the distribution). The reason for the need for greater variability can be seen from the fact that both the numerator and denominator of the t-ratio are random variables (both involve a quantity which varies from sample to sample—$\overline{X}$ in the numerator, and $S_{\overline{x}}$ in the denominator). Thus, the t-ratio will vary more than the z-ratio since the denominator of the z-score, the population standard deviation, is a constant. Thus the lack of knowledge of the population standard deviation requires the use of a sampling distribution different from that which would be used if this knowledge were available. However, as the sample size increases, the error introduced by treating S_x as σ_x and using the normal distribution as the sampling distribution instead of the t-distribution becomes small, and for (very) large samples the use of the normal distribution as the sampling distribution is quite justifiable.

If we cannot assume that the populations sampled are normally distributed, one might expect that neither the normal nor the t would be the appropriate sampling distribution. However, an important theorem in statistics, the Central Limit Theorem, comes to the rescue. From a nontechnical perspective, the Central Limit Theorem says that—irrespective of the distribution of the parent population—given that it has a mean μ and a variance σ^2, and so long as the sample size N is large, the distribution of sample means is approximately normal with mean μ and variance σ^2/N. Thus, for practical purposes, if the sample is large, little error is introduced by using the normal distribution as the sampling distribution in testing hypotheses about the mean. However, where the sample size is small, unless the population is normally distributed, it is risky to use *either* the t or the normal distribution as the sampling distribution. In these situations one ought to consider seriously the various nonparametric alternatives to the two techniques indicated above.

To illustrate the use of the t and normal distributions, assume that we have drawn a simple random sample of 25 cases from a normal population, and are testing the hypothesis

$$Ho: \mu = 15$$

against the alternative

$$H_a: \mu \neq 15$$

at the .05 level of significance.

From our sample we obtain $\bar{X} = 13.7$ and $S_X = 2.3$, where

$$S_X^2 = \Sigma(X - \bar{X})^2/(N - 1). [22]$$

Thus $S_{\bar{X}} = S_X/N^{1/2} = 2.3/5 = .46$, and $t_{24} = (13.7 - 15)/.46 = -2.83$. Since the critical value of t for a .05 level of significance and 24 degrees of freedom[23] is ±2.06 (Table 3), the calculated value of t exceeds it, and our test leads to a rejection of the null hypothesis.

If we sample again from the same population, this time taking a large sample, N = 100, and obtain $\bar{X} = 14.3$ and $S_X = 2.5$, the following calculation ensues. Note that now the sampling distribution is the normal:

$$z = (14.3 - 15)/(2.5/100^{1/2}) = -2.80.$$

Since the critical value for a test against a nondirectional hypothesis when the sampling distribution is the normal distribution is 1.96, we again reject the null hypothesis, as the test statistic is larger than the critical value.

Two Sample Tests

A more complex (in terms of procedure) hypothesis test involving means—and in general, a more likely situation for most research—is the significance test to determine if two samples have been drawn from populations with different means. In this situation the concern is not with the absolute values of the population means, but rather with the magnitude of the difference between them.

In this situation the null hypothesis is typically

$$Ho: \mu_1 - \mu_2 = 0$$

or, alternately

$$\text{Ho: } \mu_1 = \mu_2 = \mu$$

Expressed in words, the hypothesis is that there is no difference in the means of the populations sampled, or that the means of the populations are the same, or that the samples have been drawn from the same population. All of these are alternative ways of expressing essentially the same notion. (At least in the sense that the test of significance does not distinguish between them.)

The sampling distribution of the difference of means will be normal if the populations are normally distributed, or will be approximately normal if the sample sizes are (very) large, irrespective of the distribution of the population(s) sampled. So long as the samples are statistically independent, the variance of the distribution of the difference of sample means (the standard error of the sampling distribution) is the sum of the separate variances, that is, the sum of the variances estimated from the samples.

$$S^2_{\bar{x}_1 - \bar{x}_2} = S^2_{\bar{x}_1} + S^2_{\bar{x}_2} = (S^2_1/N_1) + (S^2_2/N_2)$$

where $S^2 = \Sigma(X - \bar{X})^2/(N-1)$

If we drew two samples, as indicated below, and test the null hypothesis Ho: $\mu_1 = \mu_2 = \mu$ against the nondirectional alternative Ha: $\mu_1 \neq \mu_2$, at the .05 level the computations are

Sample 1	Sample 2
N = 140	N = 210
$\bar{X}$ = 35.3	$\bar{X}$ = 33.1
S = 12.7	S = 7.2

$$S_{\bar{x}_1 - \bar{x}_2} = [(12.7^2/140) + (7.2^2/210)]^{\frac{1}{2}}$$

$$= 1.183$$

$$z = (35.3 - 33.1)/1.183$$

$$= 1.860$$

Again, since the .05 level of significance is being used, the critical value is 1.96 for a test against a nondirectional alternative. Since 1.860 is smaller than the critical value, we fail to reject the null hypothesis, and conclude that it is plausible that the samples were drawn from populations with the same mean.

In the above example, had we been able to assume that the populations sampled were normally distributed, and that the population variances were equal, the t distribution with $N_1 + N_2 - 2$ degrees of freedom would have been the appropriate sampling distribution. The advantage of being able to make *both* assumptions (normally distributed populations, equal variances) is that this allows a test of the difference of means regardless of sample size. (Note that in the discussion above, large samples had to be drawn in order to assume that the sampling distribution is normal).

Since in this case (normal populations, equal variances) the assumption is that the populations sampled have the same variances, the separate estimates of the population variance obtained from the samples are combined (pooled) to get a single estimate of the common population variance which is then used to obtain the variance estimate for the distribution of the difference of means. The formula for the pooled estimate is

$$S^2 = [(N_1 - 1)S_1^2 + (N_2 - 1)S_2^2]/(N_1 + N_2 - 2)$$

and the formula for the standard deviation of the distribution of the difference of means is

$$S_{\bar{x}_1 - \bar{x}_2} = [(S^2/N_1) + (S^2/N_2)]^{1/2} = (S^2[(1/N_1) + (1/N_2)])^{1/2}$$

where $(N_i - 1)S_i^2$ is the sum of squares for sample i, and the numerator is thus the estimate of the sum of squares for the population. Dividing the sum of squares by the degrees of freedom provides the estimate of the population variance.

Using the data for the two samples given above, assuming now that both assumptions hold for the populations (normality, equal variance), the computations are

$$S^2 = [139(12.7^2) + 209(7.2^2)]/(140 + 210 - 2)$$

$$= 95.56$$

$$S_{\bar{x}_1 - \bar{x}_2} = (95.56[(1/140) + (1/210)])^{1/2}$$

$$= 1.07$$

$$t = (35.3 - 33.1)/1.07$$

$$= 2.06$$

The result is significant at the .05 level for a t with 348 degrees of freedom, since the t-distribution is essentially identical to the normal distribution for degrees of freedom above approximately 120, and 1.96 is the critical value for the .05 level of significance. Thus, we reject the null hypothesis.

A noteworthy point in this example is that the ability to make stronger assumptions (both normality and equal variance) may result in a test with greater power as this result is significant, while the earlier result is not.

K-Sample Test

In many instances there will be a need to determine whether or not a series of samples could have been drawn from populations with the same mean or, equivalently, whether or not the samples were drawn from the same population. One approach to assessing this would be to do pairwise tests between all possible combinations of pairs of sample means. However, there are two serious problems with such an approach. One is that for more than a small number of samples, the process becomes tedious—4 samples require 6 separate tests, 7 samples require 21 separate tests, 9 samples require 36 separate tests, and so on. The other is that such a series of pairwise tests are not independent, and the nominal level of significance ("nominal level of significance" means the level of significance set for each of the separate tests—assumedly the same for all tests) is not the actual level of significance which obtains. The actual level of significance for the series of tests will be larger than the nominal level by a factor which will be related to the number of samples. In other words, the result is that a true null hypothesis (all samples came from the same population, or populations with the same mean) will be rejected more frequently than the nominal level of significance would indicate.

The appropriate procedure in this situation is an analysis of variance F-test. The F-test is a ratio of two independent estimates of the population variance obtained from the samples, and in the context of an analysis of variance will allow one to determine if the samples were drawn from the same population (or populations with the same mean). It may seem a bit odd that one can test a hypothesis about means by use of variances, but the logic underlying analysis of variance indicates that this is the case, and also why it is the case.

Since analysis of variance is the topic of another monograph in this series (see Iversen and Norpoth, 1976), we will not develop the logic of the procedure here, other than to indicate that a difference in the means of the populations sampled *biases*[24] the variance estimate that is used in the numerator of the F-ratio in the direction of being too large, while leaving the variance estimate that is used in the denominator unaffected. Thus, if the populations sampled have the same mean, both variance estimates are unbiased estimates of the same population variance, and the F-ratio should be 1, except for sampling variability. If the populations sampled have different means, the numerator will be larger than the denominator, resulting in an F-ratio larger than 1. Thus the means for detecting a false null hypothesis is available; the null hypothesis will be judged false on those occasions in which the F-ratio exceeds 1 by an amount greater than we can attribute to chance fluctuations in sampling, that is, an amount unlikely if the null hypothesis is true.

To illustrate an analysis of variance, suppose we were interested in testing the hypothesis that religious involvement differs by religious affiliation; in other words, that some faiths involve their adherents in more religiously oriented behaviors than other faiths. To test this hypothesis we draw independent, simple random samples of Catholics, Protestants, Jews, and a residual category we will call Other religions, and obtain for the respondents the number of religiously oriented behaviors engaged in per week as the measures of religious involvement. Table 12 presents the data for these samples. The null hypothesis tested is that the samples were obtained from populations with the same mean, for example:

TABLE 12
Religious Involvement by Religious Affiliation
(Hypothetical Data)

	Religious Affiliation		
Jewish	Protestant	Catholic	Other
3	5	6	9
5	4	6	0
4	4	3	8
2	3	2	8
1	1	1	4
7	1	0	3
	2	8	1
	6	5	
		7	

$$\text{Ho:}\ \mu_1 = \mu_2 = \mu_3 = \mu_4 = \mu$$

since the means of the populations must be the same if the amount of involvement is the same.

The calculations needed to obtain the test statistic involve obtaining the sums of squares (it assumed that the reader knows how to calculate a sum of squares) which, when divided by degrees of freedom provide the variance estimates for F-ratio.

The formulas for the numerator (between) sum of squares, and the denominator (within) sum of squares are:

$$NS_b^2 = \Sigma\Sigma(\bar{X}_j - \bar{X})^2 = \Sigma(\Sigma X_{ij})^2/N_j - (\Sigma\Sigma X_{ij})^2/N$$

$$NS_w^2 = \Sigma\Sigma(X_{ij} - \bar{X}_j)^2 = \Sigma\Sigma X_{ij}^2 - \Sigma(\Sigma X_{ij})^2/N_j$$

where $\bar{X}$ is the grand mean, $\bar{X}_j$ is the mean of the *jth* sample, and N_j is the number of cases in the *jth* sample. The degrees of freedom need for the variance estimates are $N-k$ (where k is the number of samples) for the denominator, and $k-1$ for the numerator.[25] The degrees of freedom for the total is the sum of these, and is $N-1$.

Substituting into the formulas above

$$NS_w^2 = 671 - 481.18 = 189.82$$

$$NS_b^2 = 481.18 - 472.03 = 9.15$$

and obtaining the total sum of squares by addition, $NS_t^2 = 189.82 + 9.15 = 198.97$, we have the quantities needed for an analysis of variance.

The analysis of variance results are presented in Table 13. If we now wish to obtain the critical value from the F-table, we enter it for 3 degrees of freedom in the numerator and 26 degrees of freedom in the denominator. (Since Table 5 does not include F-values for 26 degrees of freedom, we need to use a more complete F-table.) For the conventional .05 level the critical value is 2.98. Since the calculated F does not exceed the critical value, we fail to reject the null hypothesis.[26] Since there is no basis in this case to reject the null hypothesis, it is reasonable to continue to believe there is no difference in religious involvement among the different religious affiliations.

In order to derive the theoretical F-distribution, along with the assumption that the variance estimates in the ratio are statistically independent, it is also necessary to assume that the populations sampled are normally dis-

TABLE 13
Analysis of Variance Table for Religious Involvement
by Religious Affiliation

Source	Sum of Squares	Degrees of Freedom	Variance Estimate	F
Between Samples	9.15	3	3.0497	.418
Within Samples	189.82	26	7.3007	
	198.97	29		

tributed, and that the variances of all of the populations sampled are equal (homoscedasticity assumption). However, it has been shown that for large samples the F-test is robust with respect to the assumptions of normality of the populations, and to the homoscedasticity assumption. Thus, so long as the samples are large, it appears that these two assumptions can be violated with relative impunity.

Existence of a Relationship

A common situation in social science research is that of determining whether or not a joint frequency distribution (contingency table, cross-tabulation, bivariate frequency distribution) is evidence that the variables involved are independent in the population from which the sample was drawn. The null hypothesis tested in this situation is that the variables are independent, or more commonly, that there is no relationship between the variables. The alternative hypothesis is that the variables are related. As is always the case, the test of significance employed is used to determine if random sampling error could account for the deviation from independence observed in the sample. A statistic commonly used for this test, particularly when the data are nominal, is the χ^2 test employed earlier as a goodness of fit test, though in this application the formulation is modified slightly since we are now dealing with a two dimensional distribution

$$\chi^2 = \sum_i \sum_j (f_{o_{ij}} - f_{e_{ij}})^2 / f_{e_{ij}}$$

where, as previously, f_o represents observed frequencies, and f_e represents expected frequencies. Though usually not referred to as such, this application is also a goodness of fit test, with the theoretical distribution (expected frequencies) calculated on the assumption that the variables are independent.[27] If the variables are independent, the expected frequencies will be proportional to the marginals—in other words, each row should have the same distribution as is found in the column marginals, and each column should have the same distribution as is found in the row marginals. The formula for the calculation is

$$f_{e_{ij}} = f_{i.} f_{.j}/N$$

where $f_{i.}$ is the total for row i, and $f_{.j}$ is the total for column j.

As an example of this technique, suppose, in a study of rural residents, we wished to test the substantive hypothesis that political party preference (Democrat, Republican, Other) is a function of the nature of one's occupation (farm, nonfarm, combination). We proceed by specifying the null hypothesis that the variables are independent, that is, that there is no relation between political party preference (PPP) and the nature of the occupation (NOC), drawing a simple random sample (87 cases) from the rural population of interest to get the joint distribution presented in Table 14, and calculating the required χ^2 value. The calculation of χ^2 for this data is as follows:

$$\chi^2 = [(9 - 7.76)^2/7.76] + [(11 - 9.48)^2/9.48] + [(5 - 7.76)^2/7.76]$$

$$+ [(13 - 10.24)^2/10.24] + [(12 - 12.52)^2/12.52]$$

$$+ [(8 - 10.24)^2/10.24] + [(5 - 9)^2/9] + [(10 - 11)^2/11]$$

TABLE 14
Joint Frequency Distribution, Political Party Preference
by Nature of Occupation (Hypotetical Data)

| Nature of Occupation | Political Party Preference | | | |
	Democrat	Republican	Other	Total
Farm	9	11	5	25
Nonfarm	13	12	8	33
Combination	5	10	14	29
Total	27	33	27	87

$$+ [(14 - 9)^2/9]$$

$$= 7.32.$$

The expected frequencies calculation is straightforward, as example: $f_{e_{11}} = 27(25)/87 = 7.76$, $f_{e_{32}} = 33(29)/87 = 11$, $f_{e_{33}} = 27(29)/87 = 9$. For a joint frequency distribution, the degrees of freedom are df $= (R-1)(C-1)$ where R is the number of rows and C is the number of columns. For the data in Table 14, the degrees of freedom computation is $(3-1)(3-1) = 4$. If we test at the usual .05 level of significance, the critical value is 9.49 (see Table 4). Since the calculated χ^2 is 7.32, we fail to reject the null hypothesis that PPP and NOC are independent (that there is no relationship between PPP and NOC). For all practical considerations, then, this means that even though the sample shows some deviation from independence (shows some relationship between the variables PPP and NOC) we conclude that the two variables are unrelated in the population. One note of caution! Nowhere in the calculations made thus far have we calculated a measure of the strength of the relationship. To have an indication of the strength of the relationship in the sample data, we must calculate a measure of the strength of relationship.[28] Finally, in order to employ this technique correctly, we must meet the assumptions given in the earlier discussion of χ^2.

Regression and Correlation

Among the more common analysis procedures used by social scientists in recent years is regression and correlation analysis. Though we assume the reader is familiar with the elements of bivariate regression and correlation (we will not deal with the multivariate case), we will review some points regarding these techniques. The objective of regression analysis is to obtain the constants b_0 and b_1 for the linear equation

$$\tilde{Y}_i = b_0 + b_1 X_i,$$

where b_0 is the intercept and b_1 is the slope coefficient. The object of correlation analysis is to obtain the correlation coefficient, r_{YX}, which is generally interpreted as indicating how well the data fit the obtained regression equation. Furthermore, in a manner analogous to an analysis of variance procedure, we can split the total sum of squares for variable Y into two additive components (sums of squares, symbolized as SS), one due to the regression (explained), and one due to variation from the regression (unexplained or residual), as follows:

$$\Sigma(Y_i - \bar{Y})^2 = \Sigma(Y_i - \tilde{Y}_i)^2 + \Sigma(\tilde{Y}_i - \bar{Y})^2$$

total SS = residual SS + explained SS.

In general we are concerned with testing two hypotheses, Ho: $\rho_{YX} = 0$, and Ho: $\beta_1 = 0$, in other words the hypotheses that the correlation is zero in the population, and that the slope coefficient in the population is zero. In practice, they reduce to a single hypothesis, since for a bivariate normal population for which homoscedasticity holds (both are assumptions made in deriving the sampling distribution used, and thus underlie the significance test employed), if $\beta_1 = 0$, then $\rho_{XY} = 0$, and vice versa. The significance test employed is based on an analysis of variance table (see Table 15), and reduces to the F-ratio (or t^2, since there is only one degree of freedom for the numerator of the F-ratio): [29]

$$F_{1,N-2} = t^2_{N-2} = r^2_{YX}(N-2)/(1 - r^2_{YX}).$$

As was the case in the analysis of variance situation, the variance estimate in the numerator of the F-ratio is a biased estimate of the population variance if the null hypothesis is false, while the variance estimate in the denominator is unbiased. (Both estimates are unbiased if the null hypothesis is true.)

To illustrate the significance test for regression and correlation, we test the hypothesis that husband and wife tend to have the same amount of education. Our null hypothesis is that there is no correlation between husband and wife education, or equivalently, that the slope coefficient for

TABLE 15
Analysis of Variance Table for Regression and Correlation

Source	Sum of Squares	DF	Mean Square	F
Due to Regression	$r^2 \Sigma y^2$ *	1	$r^2 \Sigma y^2$	
Residual	$(1-r^2)\Sigma y^2$	N-2	$(1-r^2)\Sigma y /(N-2)$	$r^2(N-2)/(1-r^2)$
Total	Σy^2	N-1		

* $\Sigma y^2 = \Sigma(Y-\bar{Y})^2$

predicting wife's education from husband's (or vice versa) is zero. The data on husband and wife education for a simple random sample of 20 married couples is given in Table 16. The calculations for the analysis result in an r_{YX} of .521. Table 17 gives the analysis of variance table. The calculated F-value is the same as is found by substituting into the F-ratio formula above—$F_{1,18} = 271(18)/.729 = 6.691$. If we take the square root of the F-value, we get the equivalent t-value of 2.587. The critical F for the .05 level and 1 and 18 degrees of freedom is 4.41, and for t for the 0.5 level and 18 degrees of freedom is 1.734. Since neither the table for F or for t included in this paper provides critical values for 18 degrees of freedom, these critical values must be obtained from a larger table. Note that the appropriate value of t is the value for a test against a directional alternative, since the F-test is "one-tailed." As a result, the null hypotheses are rejected. Our conclusion is that there is a relation between husband's and wife's education, though, again, we have not proved this to be the case. (See Uslaner, 1976, for a more extended discussion of significance tests in regression analysis.)

Other Tests of Significance

It would be futile in a paper of this length to attempt to cover more than a small fraction of the possible tests of significance, so in the illustrations used, an attempt was made to emphasize the logic of the process of testing for significance. Hopefully, once the logic of the procedure is mas-

TABLE 16
Years of Education of Husband and Wife (Hypothetical Data)

Couple	(X) Husband	(Y) Wife	Couple	(X) Husband	(Y) Wife
1	7	6	11	11	13
2	7	9	12	15	14
3	12	10	13	14	10
4	11	13	14	16	16
5	10	13	15	8	8
6	5	7	16	2	8
7	9	11	17	14	8
8	11	14	18	8	12
9	11	15	19	12	16
10	12	7	20	16	12

$\Sigma X = 211,$ $\quad \Sigma Y = 222,$ $\quad \Sigma X^2 = 2481,$ $\quad \Sigma Y^2 = 2652,$ $\quad \Sigma XY = 2456$

$\Sigma (Y-\bar{Y})^2 = 187.8,$ $\qquad r_{YX} = .521,$ $\qquad b_{YX} = .447$

TABLE 17

Analysis of Variance Table for Test of Hypotheses that
$\rho_{xy} = 0, \beta_{yx} = 0$, **for Husband and Wife Education**

Source	Sum of Squares	DF	MS	F
Due to Regression	.271 (187.8) = 50.9	1	50.9/1 = 50.9	50.9/7.61 = 6.69
Residual	.729 (187.8) = 136.9	18	136.9/18=7.61	
Total	187.8	19		

tered, each new test of significance encountered will be understandable, and the learning of each new technique will be no more involved than mastering the arithmetic involved in the calculation of the required test statistic.

To summarize briefly, the proper use of a test of significance involves the following:

(1) meeting the assumptions of the technique, or knowing that the technique is robust with respect to certain assumptions, particularly assumptions about sampling, level of measurement, distribution of population, and various miscellaneous assumptions such as independence of samples, homoscedasticity, and the like;

(2) knowing the sampling distribution of the test statistic;

(3) calculating the test statistic; and

(4) comparing the test statistic with the sampling distribution to determine if the sample result is, or is not, accounted for by sampling error.

Typical, (4) is accomplished by determining if the test statistic is smaller or larger than the critical value given in the table for the sampling distribution. In most cases, we decide that sampling error cannot account for the sample result when the test statistic is larger than the critical value, as this usually means that the result is further away from the expected value, and thus less probable. However, there are a few cases where this "rule" of procedure—rejecting when the test statistic is larger than the critical value—is violated, typically in the case of certain nonparametric techniques and small samples. In these cases the test statistic must be smaller than the critical value, so *one must always be cognizant of what values of the test statistic represent unlikely sample results*, that is, results that have a low probability of occurring.

Confidence Intervals

Though the construction of confidence intervals is technically an estimation procedure rather than a significance testing procedure, there is a
relationship between the two procedures that should be explored briefly.

The usual reason for constructing a confidence interval is to obtain a
range of values such that a set proportion (called a *confidence level*, or
level of confidence) of such intervals over the long run would contain the
true population parameter. In other words, rather than being content
with the point estimate of the parameter provided by the sample statistic,
we obtain an interval that has some high probability of containing the
parameter. Essentially, we wish to calculate two values, such that there is
a high probability that the true parameter lies within the range determined
by these two values. One of the two values represents an estimate of the
largest value of the parameter for which the obtained sample statistic
would be the smallest value that would occur by chance with a probability
of ½ the level set as the level of confidence. The other represents the
smallest estimate of the parameter for which the obtained sample statistic
would be the largest value that would occur by chance with a probability
of ½ the level set as the level of confidence.

Since the verbal description of a confidence interval is rather complex,
the following illustration will help to clarify the description. In an earlier
example, a sample had been drawn to test the hypothesis that the population mean, μ, was 15. For this sample the mean was 14.3, the standard
deviation was 2.5, the standard error of the mean was .25 and the sample
size was 100. We will use this information to illustrate confidence interval
construction. Our problem is to obtain the two parameter estimates referred to above. Consider first the estimate of the parameter which would
give the sample statistic as the smallest value which would occur with a
probability of ½β (we will use β to indicate the level of confidence) if the
estimated parameter value were the true parameter value. Figure 7 presents this graphically. The problem now is one of obtaining the value of
μ_U given the information from the sample. The needed formula is obtained by solving the z-score formula for the test of significance for a
sample mean

$$z = (\bar{X} - \mu)/S_{\bar{X}}$$

for the parameter:

$$\mu = \bar{X} - zS_{\bar{X}}.$$

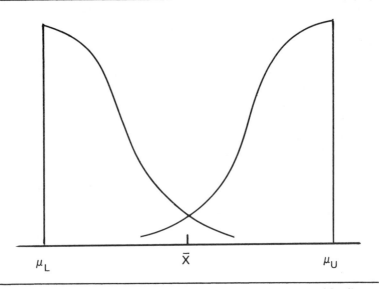

If we wish to work at the $\beta = .95$ (or 95%) level of confidence, we need a value of z (critical value) such that $\frac{1}{2}(.95)$, or .475 of the long run sample means obtained by random sampling would fall in the inclusive region $\overline{X}$ to μ_U. (We will use the symbols μ_U and μ_L to represent the Upper and Lower ends of the confidence interval.) Using Table 2, we find that the appropriate value of z is -1.96 (since $.5 - .475 = .025$, and the z corresponding to this is 1.96 and is given a negative sign since $\overline{X}$ falls in the negative end of the sampling distribution for μ_U). Substituting in the formula

$$\mu_U = 14.3 - (-1.96)(.25) = 14.79.$$

The value of μ_L is calculated in the same fashion, except that the value of z is now 1.96 since the value of $\overline{X}$ now lies in the positive side since we are considering the sampling distribution for μ_L,

$$\mu_L = 14.3 - (1.96)(.25) = 13.81$$

and the resulting .95 confidence interval is $13.81 - 14.79$. The interpretation of this interval is that .95 of the intervals calculated over the long run would contain the true mean (population mean). Unfortunately, we have no way of determining whether or not the true mean lies within this particular interval.

Since the formula for the test of significance of a mean was used as the basis for the formula for calculating the estimates of the largest and smallest values of the interval, it should be reasonably obvious that there is a relationship between significance tests and confidence intervals. Specifically, a confidence interval can be used to test any number of null hypotheses (Ho: $\mu = k$) against nondirectional alternatives (Ho: $\mu \neq k$) at a level of signficance complementary to (in other words the two values sum to 1.0) the level of confidence ($\alpha = 1.0 - \beta$). If the sample statistic falls outside the calculated confidence interval, we reject the null hypothesis, as this is the equivalent of the sample statistic falling into the region of rejection in a significance test. If the sample statistic falls within the calculated confidence interval, we fail to reject the null hypothesis, as this represents a value of the sample statistic which could occur by chance if the null hypothesis were true. To use the above example, the confidence interval just calculated could be used to test a series of null hypotheses at the .05 level of significance ($.05 = 1.00 - .95$). For example we could test the null hypotheses that the population mean is 13.0, 13.5, 14.0, 14.5, 15.0, 15.5, 16.0, and so on, against nondirectional alternative hypotheses. Thus we would reject the hypotheses that the mean is 13, 13.5, 15.0, 15.5, and 16, and we would fail to reject the rest. Notice that for the hypothesis that the mean is 15, we reached the same conclusion in this case using the confidence interval as we reached in the earlier test of significance. Obviously, by varying the level of confidence we can change the size of the interval, and also test hypotheses at levels of significance other than .05. For example, for the same data a .99 confidence interval is

$$\mu_U = 14.3 - (-2.55)(.25) = 14.94$$

$$\mu_L = 14.3 - (2.55)(.25) = 13.66$$

The null hypotheses that the mean is 13, 13.5, 15, 15.5, and 16 would also be rejected at the .01 level of significance ($.01 = 1.00 - .99$).

So long as the sampling distribution of a statistic is normal and the standard error of the statistic is known, we can calculate the upper and lower limits (parameter estimates) of the confidence interval using the formula

$$\delta = d - z_\beta S_d$$

where δ is the calculated value of some parameter estimated by the sample value d, where d is some normally distributed statistic, z_β is the normal distribution standard deviation for the selected level of confidence, and S_d is the standard error of d. The resulting interval can either be used as an indication of the possible range of values for the parameter, or can be used to test null hypotheses against nondirectional alternatives at a level of significance complementary to the level of confidence.

The Interpretation of Significance Tests

The test of significance has become an integral part of the research process in most empirically oriented social science disciplines. Yet, there have been a number of serious questions raised as to the utility and sensibility of employing significance tests in social research (Morrison and Henkel, 1970). Before examining some of these questions, we will summarize a number of points about tests of significance. It is important to recognize the fact that probability theory, on which tests of significance are based, is a part of the discipline of pure mathematics, and as such is a formal model which can be interpreted in different ways. The procedures and interpretations we call tests of significance are only one of the applications and interpretations of mathematical models of random behavior. Other interpretations will be discussed later.

The correctness of probability estimates obtained through the use of a test of significance are a function of the extent to which the assumptions which underlie the techniques are met by the data on which the test is performed, unless the test has been shown by either empirical or theoretical analysis to be robust with regard to assumptions not well met by the data. In particular, the correctness of the probability estimates is contingent on the appropriateness of the sampling procedure used, as the nature of the random or chance factors affecting the data are a function of the sampling procedures. Since the sampling distribution of any test statistic is based on particular models of random behavior, in which the random behavior is "produced" by the appropriate sampling procedure, varying the sampling procedure "produces" different random behavior and a different sampling distribution than the distribution assumed. Hence, the probability estimate obtained, when the sampling procedure is different from that assumed by a particular technique, has a high probabilty of being in error, though how much in error one generally can not specify. Most certainly, if the sampling procedure is nonrandom (due to nonresponse, a nonprobability design, or whatever) the probability calculation has no meaning in the sense of classical statistical inference (where the interest is on statistically generalizing from the sample to the population sampled), though other interpretations of the random process model may be appropriate.

Tests of significance provide an indication of the probability with which a particular sample result, or a more extreme result (in other words, one further away from the expected value of the distribution) would occur if the null hypothesis were true. Thus the obtained probability is based on a hypothetical situation—that the null hypothesis is true. Consequently the test provides no information about the probability of the particular result occurring if some other situation is true.

Depending on the tables available for the sampling distribution utilized, the information on the probability of the particular sample result may be more or less precise. If the tables for the sampling distribution only provide critical values for selected levels of significance, say every fifth percentile, or for just the .05, .01, and .001 levels as is often the case for the F-distribution, the information on the probability of the obtained sample result is quite imprecise. Unless interpolation is possible, one can only establish the fact that the sample result is either more probable or less probable than the probability set as the level of significance. If interpolation is possible, the precision of the probability obtained is dependent on the size of the interval over which the interpolation is made and the characteristics of the distribution in that interval (mainly the change in the slope of the curve bounding the distribution). Additionally, many sampling distributions for statistics are *only approximated* by the theoretical distributions used as the sampling distribution.

Since a particular significance test is typically employed a single time, the notion of the probability of a particular sample result occurring requires that one construct (mentally) another hypothetical situation, the situation in which a large number (infinite number) of replications of the study—sampling, data analysis, and so on—are carried out so that it is possible to think of probability in terms of a relative frequency. In other words, we have to think of the particular study as one of a large number of identical studies, so that the notion of a sampling distribution is relevant. Thus one may well question the sensibility of making important decisions on a theoretical formulation on the basis of a single test, since the probability we obtain relates to a hypothetical construct—a hypothetical population of replications of the study.

The choice of significance level at which to work is an arbitrary decision since neither substantive theory nor statistical theory dictate that a particular level of significance be used. It is true that in certain circumstances, such as quality control situations, a rational basis for both the Type I error (level of significance) and the Type II error can be established on the basis of minimizing the economic costs of making either type of error. However, since it is impossible to establish the costs of making an incorrect decision with regard to scientific theories, there is only a subjective, arbitrary basis for any level of significance chosen, even if the level chosen is either of the conventional levels—.05 or .01.

The results of a test of significance have relevance only to the population from which the sample was drawn in conformity with the requirements of the appropriate sampling design (invariably it must be simple random sampling). Inferences to other populations, populations not sampled, cannot be made on statistical grounds.[30]

Simply summarized, the test of significance provides the probability (with varying degrees of precision) that a particular unique event (the particular sample result), or a more extreme event, would occur in a hypothetical situation which has three components—the null hypothesis is true, the study can be thought of as one of a very large sequence of identical studies, and the various assumptions underlying the test are met by the data, or have been shown empirically or theoretically to be unimportant for the valid interpretation of the results of the technique.

Thus, the test of significance is a particular implementation of a probability model, or model of random behavior, with a restricted interpretation. The question now posed is how relevant is the test of significance to social research?

Questions of the Utility of Tests of Significance

The problems with the use of tests of significance in social science research can be viewed from two perspectives. The first perspective is concerned with the correspondence between the mathematical model and its assumptions, on which tests of significance are based, and the reality to which the model is applied. In other words, do the characteristics of the data to which tests of significance are applied correspond to the characteristics assumed by the mathematical model? The second perspective is concerned with the question of whether, even if there is a close correspondence between the characteristics of the data and the characteristics assumed by the mathematical model, the use of tests of significance contributes to the goal of science. Thus, the first of these perspectives is concerned with questions of a technical nature, and the second perspective is concerned with issues of a philosophy of science nature.

These perspectives are not mutually exclusive, as questions of a technical nature may have implications for, or become questions of a philosophy of science nature in certain contexts, and vice versa. However, it is useful to make the analytic distinction between the two perspectives.

Technical Issues

First we shall consider some of the technical arguments against the use of tests of significance. We will limit this discussion to problems arising out of sampling procedures, power, and choice of significance level, though other technical issues—the use of improper techniques, data dredging, improper interpretations of results, and the like—are serious problems. However, these latter are problems that can be overcome by better training in the use of tests of significance, while the problems to be discussed are less amenable to solution by better training. In fact, given the state of development in most social sciences, these technical problems in the use of tests of significance may not be solvable, at least not in the near future.

Sampling Issues: The sampling distributions used in virtually all tests of significance require that simple random samples be drawn from the populations to which the statistical generalization is to be made. The use of any other sampling procedure results in a sampling distribution different from the sampling distribution produced by simple random sampling, though at this time no general rules can be given for the manner in which alterations in the sampling procedure alter the sampling distribution. Thus the error introduced into the probability calculations by the use of sampling distributions based on simple random sampling assumptions when the sampling procedure is a probability sampling procedure, but not simple random sampling, is usually unknown. There are no simple, universally available guidelines to enable the estimation of the size and direction of the error in the probability calculations. The error may be minimal in some cases, but serious in others (Kish, 1957: 156, 164; 1965: 576). The problem is usually much more serious in the case of what are often called analytical studies—studies in which the focus is on bivariate or multivariate statistics—since it is difficult, if not impossible, to derive sampling distributions for analytic statistics when nonsimple random sampling has been used, particularly when the sampling procedure is complex (some combination of probability sampling procedures).

There is a very serious question of the utility of employing significance tests in social research since it is unlikely, for the following two reasons, that one will obtain a simple random sample:

(1) it is unusual, to say the least, to have a complete list of the elements in a nontrivial population (one which is large enough and varied enough to be relevant to the testing of theoretical formulations), and

(2) it is unusual to obtain a high response rate from the sample elements chosen.

Without playing down the problem of not having the basic requisite for drawing a simple random sample, the list of the population, we wish to emphasize a point that is often overlooked in conjunction with nonresponse.

That point is that when the nonresponse rate is as high as it often is in social research (for an extreme example, a return rate on mailed questionnaires of less than 60% is not unusual), the high nonresponse rate results in a sample that must be considered to be a nonprobability sample. The employment of significance tests on such a sample is nonsensical as there is no way that only random error has affected the statistics calculated from the sample. It makes no sense to attempt to make statistical inferences from nonprobability samples to existing populations.

Before taking up a final topic on sampling, the use of random subsampling, it should be obvious that the tone of this section has been generally negative to the use of tests of significance on samples obtained in most social research projects, as it is very unlikely that the samples are truly simple random samples, and that as a result the probability estimates obtained through the use of formulas assuming simple random sampling will be incorrect by some unknown amount. Yet, the history of statistics (in fact, mathematics in general) is replete with examples of cases where techniques have been shown, sooner or later, to be quite insensitive to violations of assumptions, and cases where results of adequate precision could be obtained through approximations that were quite crude compared to the correct procedures. Thus there is ample precedent for contending that too much concern for assumptions may be unwarranted. Thus samples that (from a strictly technical perspective) are not simple random samples, but are reasonable approximations—simple random samples with small nonresponse rates, simple random samples drawn from an incomplete list of the population but a list containing at least some cases of all types that are of interest to the study, et cetera—might possibly be treated as simple random samples with little error resulting. However, the extent to which such an approach is successful must be a function of sophistication and mature judgment, qualities not uniformly distributed among researchers.

Random Subsampling: With the advent of fairly easy access to large-scale computers, techniques which have been under development through the last three or so decades are providing ways of avoiding some of the problems of statistical inference for nonsimple random probability samples. Though the techniques included in this approach are sufficiently different, complex, and involved to preclude detailed discussion here, the basic idea that underlies the various techniques is that subsamples may be drawn from an existing sample, various statistics may be calculated for the subsamples, and the resulting values for the statistics may be used, among other things, to empirically determine (as opposed to mathematically derive) sampling distributions and characteristics of sampling distributions. There are quite a number of factors which complicate the use of this subsampling approach—the nature of the original sample, the subsampling procedure, the nature of the data (artificial, real), the availability of computer programs, and the like—and as a result, the approach has been relatively little used in the social sciences, though its potential would seem to be great. In any event, the use of an appropriate subsampling technique provides a means of getting around some of the problems of using non-simple random probability samples in statistical inference providing one has access to adequate computer facilities. The reader who wishes more information on the approach should consult Finifter (1972) for a relatively nontechnical survey.

Power: The notion of the power of a test has been discussed earlier, though its importance to significance testing has not been considered. The power of a test, from a nontechnical perspective, is the ability of the test to detect a false null hypothesis. Since the null hypotheses tested in social science research are usually hypotheses believed to be false (set up to be rejected, or specifying parameters of zero, a highly unlikely situation) tests of such hypotheses should be set up so that there is a high probability of their rejection. Yet, in most social science research, there is no way to determine the probability of rejecting a false null hypothesis, that is, no way to determine the power of the test, since this determination is based on an ability social scientists seem to lack—the ability to specify a point hypothesis as the alternative against which we are testing. (Since we never know the true value for the parameter, power has to be considered relative to a specified alternative.)

Since the power of a test is always equal to or greater than the level of significance when the null hypothesis is in fact false (at least in the cases common in the social science research where the region of rejection is always placed in the tails of the sampling distributions), there is some consolation in knowing that when testing at the .05 level there is at least a .05 probability of detecting a false null hypothesis. However, without a knowledge of the true state of affairs, one cannot be sure that the null hypothesis is false (in the sense that the difference between the parameter value specified in the null hypothesis and the true value for the parameter is substantively important), even though one may believe it to be false. And, without a realistic point alternative against which to test the null, there is no way to estimate the probability of detecting the fact that the null hypothesis is false, if it is false. It seems rather nonscientific to subject a hypothesis believed to be false to a test that may have a probability of rejecting the hypothesis that is not much greater (though unknown) than that set as the level of significance.

Finally, a point often overlooked, is that finding or failing to find a significant result is often more a function of sample size than the intrinsic truth or falsity of the null hypothesis. This results from the fact that a major component of the power of a test is the size of the sample—power increasing as sample size increases. For a large enough sample, almost any deviation from the null hypothesis will result in a statistically significant result. One of the simplest techniques which can be used to demonstrate this is chi-square. It can be shown (Blalock, 1972: 293) that if we multiply each frequency in a contingency table by some constant value k, the value of chi-square is multiplied by the same constant. Thus we can set up a proportion table (proportions based on total N) which exhibits a very weak (even by social science standards) relationship, and by varying the sample size by some factor k_i show that there will be some value of k which will produce statistical significance, *even though the strength of the relationship is not altered by increasing sample size.* For example, for Table 18 the value of ϕ (phi) is .0445 and is likely to be interpreted as indicating essentially no relationship.[31] If we were to test for significance at the .05 level, the critical value for chi-square with 1 degree of freedom is 3.84 (see Table 4). If the sample size is 100 (that is, if all the proportions in the table below are multiplied by 100) the resulting chi-square is .1984, and is not significant. If the sample size is 1000, the value of chi-square is 1.984, still not significant. If the sample size is 2000, the result is 3.968, and is significant at the .05 level. If the sample size is increased to slightly less than 3,500 the result will be significant at the .01 level. Yet, while the value of chi-square increases with sample size, the value of phi remains constant, therefore, the strength of the relationship is unchanged. Thus, had the null hypothesis of no relationship in fact been false, tests of significance based on small samples (in this case anything much smaller than 2000) would not have determined this to be the case. On the other hand, had the null hypothesis been true, samples of over 2000 would have led the researcher to conclude otherwise. The moral of

TABLE 18
Hypothetical 2 x 2 Proportion Distribution for Illustrating the Effect of Sample Size on Power

.19	.41	.60
.11	.29	.40
.30	.70	1.00

this is that an essentially arbitrary factor, the sample size, can often determine the conclusion reached in a test of significance which is mechanically applied and interpreted.

Arbitrary Level of Significance: In social science research the typical procedure in hypothesis testing is to test null hypotheses that are believed to be false, in the hope of rejecting them so that the research hypothesis can be accepted. Failure to reject the null hypothesis generally leads to the conclusion that the research hypothesis is false, and further study of the relationship involved in the research hypothesis is discontinued. Several aspects of this process should give the intelligent researcher pause for thought. The level of significance at which one chooses to work is very clearly critical to which null hypotheses are rejected (and work continues on the research hypothesis), and which are not (and work stops on the research hypothesis). Since the choice of a level of significance at which to work is not based in any mathematical, statistical, or substantive theory, the choice of a significance level is totally arbitrary, at least in basic research where there is no rational procedure by which one can attach a cost to either the Type I or Type II error. The absurdity of adhering rigidly to arbitrary significance levels has to be apparent to the thoughtful researcher, as it substitutes a mechanical procedure for mature, scientific judgment. In addition to the fact that the level of significance is arbitrary, one has also to consider the fact that the power of a test is usually unknown; to discontinue research on a particular relationship when the test's ability to detect a false null hypothesis is unknown again seems nonscientific. Also, unless one is cognizant of, and has controlled for the effects of possible suppressor variables (Rosenberg, 1973) on the phenomena involved in the hypothesis, the results of tests of significance can be quite misleading. The research hypothesis may in fact be true, but this fact may be concealed by the effects of suppressor variables not controlled. Thus, the reliance on the test of significance to indicate hypotheses deserving of continued study can become a bar to creative theoretical thinking.

Philosophy of Science Issues

The more serious questions about the utility of the use of tests of significance in social science research revolve around the contribution of tests of significance to the goal of science. The goal of science is the development and validation of theories that enable the explanation, prediction, and/or control of empirical phenomena. The validation of theories results not so much from proving them to be true, but by repeated testing which fails to refute them. Our belief in the validity of theories is the result of a cognitive process, and results in a degree of belief in the theories rather than a decision that the theory is either right or wrong. The theories, themselves, refer to a hypothetical universe—hypothetical in the sense that it encompasses all past, present, and future cases to which the theory applies, wherever they may occur. Thus, philosophy of science issues have to do with the nature of the information provided, generalizability of results, the nature of the hypotheses tested, and the cumulative nature of science.

Nature of Information Provided: The nature of the information provided by a test of significance is at odds with the needs of science. Since hypotheses can not be proven true in a single test, they provide at best negative information, and result in a decision to reject or fail to reject a theoretical statement, rather than resulting in an adjustment, an increase or decrease, in our degree of belief in the theoretical statement.

Generalizability: Tests of significance do not allow generalizations to the hypothetical population of interest. Since statistical inferences are limited to the population from which the simple random sample was drawn, there is no way to make a *statistical inference* to the population to which the theory applies, as it is impossible to draw a simple random sample from a nonexistent portion of the hypothetical population. Thus any generalizations to the hypothetical population of interest must be made on extra-statistical grounds. Furthermore, it is very unusual to draw a simple random sample from even the totality of that portion of the hypothetical universe which is available, since samples are usually drawn from only that portion of the existing portion of the hypothetical universe which is close at hand.

Nature of the Null Hypothesis: The nature of the null hypotheses typically tested in social science research leaves much to be desired. For the most part they posit parameters of zero. Since it is unlikely that parameters of interest will be precisely zero, rejecting such hypotheses is not very informative. Furthermore, as Meehl (1967) has indicated, the usual procedure for corroborating theories—by refuting null hypotheses—has a high prior probability of corroborating the theory, even if the theory is false, and the basic factor leading to this state of affairs is the fact that the null hypotheses tested do not posit specific, or point, values other than zero. (More precisely, Meehl's conclusion is that the prior probability of rejecting a directional null hypothesis approaches .5, irrespective of the truth or falsity of the hypothesis, as the power of the test is increased toward unity.)

Cumulative Nature of Science: Finally, scientific knowledge is cumulative. Yet, the test of significance model makes no use of information garnered by prior tests of the same hypothesis. Each test of a hypothesis is an independent, isolated event. Even if one were inclined to include in a particular test the information from prior tests—say that out of 20 prior tests of the hypothesis, it was rejected eight times and not rejected the remaining 12—the standard test of significance model could not incorporate that information. This is not to say that there are no probability models available which could incorporate such information, but to say that the typical tests of significance—the *t*-test for a difference of means, or the chi-square test of independence, for example—do not. Thus, the believer in the utility of tests of significance is in the peculiar position of either having to repeat the test of significance for a particular hypothesis whenever someone wishes to know whether the hypothesis is true or false, or having to concede that a single test of the hypothesis determines once and for all time the truth or falsity of a hypothesis. Surely most researchers would find either solution unacceptable, but to do so implies that the test of significance is essentially irrelevant to the purpose of basic scientific research—or if not irrelevant, surely of very little importance.

Other Interpretations

As was indicated earlier, the mathematical models of random behavior, or probability models that we call significance tests, can be interpreted in different ways. What we have called the classical statistical inferential (test of significance) interpretation of the probability model assumes that the source of randomness is in the sampling process, nowhere else, and that we are working with a probability sample from some well-defined, existent universe. However, we may wish to apply tests of significance to data we assume constitute a population. (The data may be the result of a complete enumeration—such as a census—or be the result of some nonrandom sampling procedure.) In this context we cannot interpret our tests of significance as though they were dealing with random sampling errors resulting from sampling from an existent population. However, there are at least three interpretations which have been advanced as meaningful interpretations when tests of significance are applied to populations and nonprobability samples.

The first of these is that our data can be thought of as a random sample from some hypothetical universe composed of data elements like those at hand. Put another way, the sample is used to define the population. Such a hypothetical population is only conceptual—it does not exist, and any statistical inference made applies only to this hypothetical nonexistent population. The question which we assume is answered by the use of a test of significance in this situation is: if such a population were to exist, could sampling error account for any differences between the expected and observed value of the statistic?

The second interpretation that one might make is that the source of randomness in the data is random measurement error. The question which we assume is answered by the use of a test of significance in this situation is: could random measurement error account for any divergence of the sample value from the expected, or hypothesized parameter? A "significant" result in this case is one in which the sample value differs from the expected value by an amount sufficiently large as to be judged unexplainable in terms of random measurement error. (In other words, the results were due to some substantively important causal factor.)

The third interpretation one might make is based on the assumption that the data were generated by some unspecified random process. The type of question we might assume is answered by a test of significance in this case is: could the obtained results have been produced by "chance" or by "accident" (without ever specifying what is meant by these phrases)? A "significant" result in this case would lead one to look for an explanation other than chance, or random behavior. In other words, rejecting the null hypothesis in this situation would be taken as an indication that some causal factor, some theoretically important factor, was involved in producing the difference between the observed value and 'the value expected under the null hypothesis that random factors produced the observed value (Gold, 1969).

Clearly, since we may make any assumptions we please, any of the above interpretations are in some sense, legitimate. However, if a simple random sampling procedure has been employed in obtaining the sample, we are *guaranteed* that chance or random factors have been allowed to operate, and we can predict the long run effect of these factors. On the other hand, the other interpretations rest on constructions existing only in our minds (that is, the hypothetical universe), or conjectures (that chance factors have, in fact, affected our data, and affected the data in a manner predictable for the long run). These interpretations may be legitimate and meaningful if they inform us about the real world, but the information they convey is a function of the correspondence between the real world conditions and the assumptions made. One should not reject these interpretations out of hand, as there may be situations in which it makes sense to test for the effects of random measurement error, or to test to see whether the data are such that a random process could have accounted for them. However opinion is quite divided on the meaningfulness of these possible interpretations.

Arguments for Tests of Significance

Oddly, it is more difficult to find specific arguments supporting the use of significance tests than it is to find arguments decrying their use. Part of the reason for this state of affairs is undoubtedly the sense that is obvious why tests of significance are useful, thus little effort has been directed to the detailing of supportive arguments.

Perhaps the most general and consistently advanced supportive argument is that tests of significance are a means of guarding against according substantive importance to results which can easily be explained by "chance," whatever the source of the chance factors—sampling, measurement error, and so on. Scientists have an almost morbid fear of attributing a causal explanation to some phenomenon, only to have it later demonstrated that the phenomenon was due to the workings of chance. Tests of significance do provide some assurance, in the form of significant results, that chance has been ruled out as an explanation.

A related argument is that the use of tests of significance provides a standard for the evaluation of findings across diverse studies, since probabilities are "pure numbers." Since probability values are pure numbers, unencumbered by diverse units or meanings, they provide an ideal mechanism for standardization, as their meanings are uniformly understood. The adoption of conventional probability levels, such as the .01 and .05, provides a uniform and easily applied standard for determining, if nothing else, which results do not seem to merit further consideration.

Conclusion

In this paper we have developed the logic of tests of significance; we have illustrated their use through a number of techniques; and we have suggested that the understanding of the logic and the procedures of tests of significance allows easy transfer of knowledge to the learning of new techniques. We have discussed the interpretations of tests of significance in the context of simple random sampling, in the context of populations and nonprobability samples, and we have shown their relation to confidence intervals. Finally, we have indicated which assumptions are important to the interpretation of the selected techniques, and some of the assumptions which can be ignored.

We have also presented some of the issues in the controversy surrounding the use of tests of significance in social science research. Though the material presented on these issues is mostly negative regarding the use of tests of significance, the reader is cautioned that the negative perspective is only one side of the controversy. There is another side, with a large number of adherents (possibly the majority of researchers), that views the use of significance tests as an integral and important aspect of scientific research. Though the author does not view the use of tests of significance in a positive light,[32] the utility of tests of significance in social science research is an issue over which reasonable persons may disagree, and certainly each reader must reach his or her conclusions regarding the utility of tests of significance in their own research.

NOTES

1. The most notable other interpretation of probability is that a probability represents a degree of belief, credibility, or confidence. In this sense, a probability is thought of as an estimate of the likelihood that a statement is true. Thus the statement—"The probability that Napoleon died of arsenic poisoning is .98"—reflects one's confidence in the conclusion regarding the cause of Napoleon's death. For a more extensive discussion of this perspective see Messic (1968), particularly the articles by Ayer, Carnap, Cohen, and Kac.

2. On any single trial we will obtain either a success or a failure, and the short run results of a series of trials need not equal or even approximate the long run probability. Put another way, it is fallacious to assume, as many gamblers do, that a run of unfavorable results makes a favorable outcome more probable. To assume that "the law of averages" guarantees that even the short run relative frequencies should approximate the long run relative frequency is to fall heir to what has often been called the Monte Carlo fallacy. So long as trials are independent, probabilities do not change from trial to trial.

3. The distinction between probability density functions and probability distributions arises from the difference between graphs representing frequency for discrete and continuous variables. For discrete variables, so long as the histogram representing the values of the variable uses uniform classes, frequency is obtainable from the height of the graph. For continuous variables this is not the case. The frequency in the range $a - b$ for continuous variables is found from the *area* under the graph between the values of a and b.

4. The simple fact that sampling on a probability basis is assumed does not guarantee that the sampling distribution of any statistic calculated from such a sample is known. It is a necessary, but not sufficient condition. The sufficient condition is that the theoretical probability distribution for the statistic has been mathematically derived on the assumption of probability sampling.

5. By robust we mean that the violation of an assumption does not materially affect the calculated probability (significance level). In other words, the effect on the sampling distribution of the statistic is minimal.

6. Another term which means, generally, the same thing as "probability sample" is "random sample." However, some care needs to be exercised when interpreting the term "random sample" as some authors have used the term to mean the same as the more specific term "simple random sample" rather than the more general "probability sample."

7. The more common of these are stratified, cluster, and systematic, with the term "complex" applied to designs which incorporate more than one of the various

procedures, including simple random sampling. For an elementary discussion of sampling, see Blalock (1972); for a more advanced discussion, see Kish (1965).

8. The degrees of freedom reflect the number of values in a distribution which are free to vary after certain constraints have been imposed—in other words, the degrees of freedom are the number of independent values in the distribution. The constraints are the number of relations specified among the values. For example, we might impose the constraint that the sum of a set of values is fixed. In this case, for a sample of N values, only the first $N-1$ of the values are independent, since the last value must be the difference between the fixed sum and the sum of the first $N-1$ values. In general, the rationale for the degrees of freedom will vary from technique to technique, so we will give both an explanation at an intuitive level and a formula for the calculation.

9. The most common applications of chi-square are situations in which the data are counts (frequencies) of the occurrence of cases in categories of some variable, or counts of joint occurrence when considering bivariate frequency distributions.

10. A test statistic is a statistic that is used in conjunction with a sampling distribution to determine the probability of a particular sample result. A test statistic is generally not considered to be a descriptive statistic since it is not in itself a parameter estimate, though its calculation is usually based on one or more descriptive statistics (parameter estimates).

11. The position indicated is often associated with the philosophy of Karl Popper (1959, 1965). There are other philosophical positions on the manner in which verified knowledge comes about, positions associated with Carnap (1953), N. R. Hanson (1958), and others.

12. The logic would be compelling if the null and the alternative hypotheses specified were mutually exclusive and exhaustive of the possibilities, and one or the other could be eliminated. However, this is never possible in nontrivial situations, so the logic indicated is faulty.

13. Often the normal distribution is used to approximate sampling distributions in situations in which a one tailed test is being made in terms of the original test statistic—such as for large degrees of freedom when the normal distribution is used to approximate the chi-square distribution. In these situations a one tailed test should be made in terms of the normal distribution as well.

14. It is not clear that, except for completeness and pedagogical reasons, discussions of Type II errors are of value in nondecision theory applications of tests of significance. Bakan (1966) makes the point that the Type II error is possible only when the null hypothesis is accepted—a technically incorrect procedure in terms of the discusssion of the fallacy of affirming the consequent. Thus, it is not clear that in the manner tests of significance are typically used in social science research, that a Type II error is possible, since the null hypothesis is not accepted. However, even if we were to admit that null hypotheses can be accepted, it is not clear that a discussion of Type II errors is of value in social science, since the Type II error can be calculated only if the alternative hypothesis is a point hypothesis, and this is an extremely rare situation in social science research.

15. The calculation of the power of a test requires two point hypotheses since the sampling distributions must be obtained for the values of the parameters specified in both hypotheses, and these sampling distributions cannot be obtained unless point values are specified for the parameters. Some sense of why both sampling distributions are needed can be gained from the discussion of power in the example of significance tests based on the binomial distribution (see Comparing Whole Distributions, in section 4).

16. Since there are k categories, and a fixed N, only $k-1$ of the category frequencies are free to vary, since the frequency in the last category must be the difference between N and the sum of frequencies in the first $k-1$ categories. Thus there are $k-1$ degrees of freedom. (The degrees of freedom can also be justified on the basis of the fact that the sum of the differences between the observed and expected frequencies must equal zero. Thus with k categories, only $k-1$ of these differences are free to vary, since the last difference must make the sum zero.)

17. The values of k given are for one tailed tests since chi-square is a one tailed test (see Conover, 1971: 397).

18. Sequential categories differing in the same direction from the expected will have a different effect on the cumulative distribution than sequential categories differing in opposite directions from the expected, and will thus affect the Kolmogorov-Smirnov test while chi-square will be unaffected by the pattern since chi-square is affected only by the magnitude of the difference from the expected.

19. As a general note, this type of correction for continuity can be applied anywhere the normal, or other continuous distribution is used to approximate a discrete distribution. However, except for the binomial case, it is unusual to see the correction as part of a formula, as it is often the case that as the number of rectangles in the histogram representing the discrete distribution increases, the increase in the precision of the result is so small as to be inconsequential.

20. The difference between this form of the z-score transformation and earlier examples is that this is a specific instance of the general form. Here the statistic is the sample mean, $\overline{X}$, the expected value of $\overline{X}$ is the population mean, μ, and the standard deviation of the sampling distribution of means is $\sigma_{\overline{X}}$.

21. We are following the general statistical practice of indicating parameters by letters of the Greek alphabet, and sample statistics by letters of the Roman alphabet.

22. The sample variance (S^2) is obtained by dividing the sum of squares by $N-1$ rather than N. The reason for this is that the expected value of S^2 is equal to the population variance if the divisor of the sum of squares is $N-1$, but not if the divisor is N (see note 24).

23. Since the sum of the deviations around the mean must be zero, for N cases, only $N-1$ of the values are free to vary, thus $N-1$ degrees of freedom (Kenney and Keeping, 1954: 183).

24. An estimator, that is, a statistic used to estimate a parameter, is biased if its expected value is different from the parameter. The expected value of an unbiased estimator is equal to the parameter value. Statisticians consider it to be a desirable characteristic of an estimator that it be unbiased.

25. For each sample, the situation indicated in note 23 must hold. Thus for the within variance estimate (denominator) there will be $N-k$ degrees of freedom. Similarly, for the between variance estimates only $k-1$ of the sample means are free to vary since the grand mean is fixed.

26. Any time the calculated F is less than 1 (the expected value of F if the null hypothesis is true is 1), there is no need to look up the critical value, as the critical value will always be greater than 1. Thus values of F less than 1 lead automatically to the decision to fail to reject the null hypothesis.

27. From the earlier definition of independence, two events are independent if the probability of their joint occurrence is equal to the product of their separate probabilities. Thus if our events are obtaining a value i on the row variable (a case falling in category i), and a value j on the column variable, the two separate probabilities are $f_{i.}/N$, and $f_{.j}/N$ respectively. In other words, the probabilities are simply

the proportions of cases in the respective categories. By definition, then, the joint occurrence of a case having the value i on the row variable and the value j on the column variable is

$$(f_i./N)(f_{.j}/N) = f_i. f_{.j}/N^2.$$

To convert this probability to an expected frequency requires multiplying it by N, resulting in the calculation $f_i. f_{.j}/N$.

28. Several measures of association, such as the coefficient of contingency and Cramer's V, are based on chi-square, and could be easily calculated since the chi-square value is available. However, chi-square based measures of association have fallen into disuse as a result of what have been called proportional reduction in error (PRE) measures, so it is more likely that a PRE measure such as Goodman's and Kruskal's tau or lambda would be calculated for nominal level data, or Somer's *d* or Goodman's and Kruskal's gamma would be computed for ordinal data.

29. The $N-2$ degrees of freedom result from the fact that in order to calculate the regression equation, two constants must be calculated—the slope and intercept coefficients—and one degree of freedom is lost for each constant.

30. This is no way intended to imply that one cannot generalize beyond the population sampled. *It is only that statistical inference cannot be used as a basis for such a generalization.* Generalizations may be made, legitimately, on the basis of the assumed or demonstrated representativeness of the sample analysed. Science is "self correcting," that is, any well documented study can be replicated, and the positive or negative results of the replication will either increase or decrease faith in the earlier generalization, usually in time to the point where incorrect generalizations are recognized as such. Thus any researcher who feels that the results of a study can be generalized beyond the population from which the sample was drawn, whether the sample is a probability sample or not, has the scientific responsibility to make the generalization, but also has the responsibility of clearly and completely stating the basis on which the generalization has been made. This may include explicitly stating the bases for the assumed representativeness of the sample.

31. The formula for phi (ϕ) is

$$\phi = (ad - bc)/((a + b)(a + c)(d + b)(d + c))^{1/2}$$

where the letters represent the cell frequencies according to the following scheme:

a	b	a + b
c	d	c + d
a + c	b + d	N

32. It appears to the author that until social science theorizing advances far beyond its present state, until problems related to sampling are resolved, and until measurement error problems are more adequately dealt with, tests of significance, if used as in the past by social scientists, will prove to be more detrimental than advantageous to the advance of the social sciences—at least at the level of basic, as contrast to applied research.

[92]

REFERENCES

BAKAN, D. (1966) "The test of significance in psychological research." Psychological Bul. 66 (December): 423-437.

BLALOCK, H. M., Jr. (1972) Social Statistics. (Sec. ed.) New York: McGraw-Hill.

CARNAP, R. (1953) "Testability and meaning," pp. 47-92 in H. Feigl and M. Brodbeck (eds.) Readings in the Philosophy of Science. New York: Appleton-Century-Crofts.

CONOVER, W. (1971) Practical Nonparametric Statistics. New York: Wiley.

COPI, I. M. (1953) Introduction to Logic. New York: Macmillan.

FINIFTER, B. (1972) "The generation of confidence: evaluating research findings by random subsample replication," pp. 112-175 in H. Costner (ed.) Sociological Methodology 1972. San Francisco: Jossey-Bass.

FISHER, R. A. (1925) Statistical Methods for Research Workers. London: Oliver & Boyd.

FRANKEL, M. (1971) Inference from survey Samples. Ann Arbor : Litho Crafters.

GARDNER, M. (1976) "Mathematical games." Scientific American 234 (March): 119-122.

GOLD, D. (1969) "Significance tests and substantive significance." American Sociologist 4 (February): 42-46.

HANSON, N. R. (1958) Patterns of Discovery. Cambridge: Univ. Press.

HAYS, W. L. (1973) Statistics for the Social Sciences. New York: Holt, Rinehart & Winston.

––– (1963) Statistics for Psychologists. New York: Holt, Rinehart & Winston.

HOGBEN, L. T. (1957) Statistical Theory: The Relationship of Probability, Credibility and Error. An Examination of the Contemporary Crisis in Statistical Theory from a Behaviorist Viewpoint. New York: Norton.

IVERSEN, G. and H. NORPOTH (1976) Analysis of Variance. In this series.

KAUFMAN, H. (1944) Prestige Classes in a New York Rural Community. Cornell University AES.

KENNEY, J. and E. KEEPING (1954) Mathematics of Statistics. New York: Van Nostrand.

KISH, L. (1965) Survey Sampling. New York: Wiley.

––– (1957) "Confidence intervals for clustered samples." Amer. Soc. Rev. 22 (April): 154-165.

KNETZ, W. J. (1963) An Empirical Study of the Effects of Selected Variables upon the Chi-Square Distribution. Washington: Amer. Institute for Research.

MEEHL, P. E. (1967) "Theory testing in psychology and physics: a methodological paradox." Philosophy of Science, 34 (June): 103-115.

MESSIC, D. M. (1968) Mathematical Thinking in the Behavioral Sciences. San Francisco: Freeman.

MORRISON, D. and R. E. HENKEL (1970) The Significance Test Controversy. Chicago: Aldine.

POPPER, K. (1965) Conjectures and Refutations. New York: Harper & Row.

––– (1959) The Logic of Scientific Discovery. New York: Basic Books.

ROSENBERG, M. (1973) "The logical status of suppressor variables." Public Opinion Q. 37 (Fall): 359-372.

USLANER, E. M. (1976) Regression Analysis: Simultaneous Equation Estimation. In this series.